Space Dogs

Space Dogs

Pioneers of Space Travel

by Chris Dubbs

Writer's Showcase

New York Lincoln Shanghai

Space Dogs
Pioneers of Space Travel

Writer's Showcase
an imprint of iUniverse, Inc.

For information address:
iUniverse, Inc.
2021 Pine Lake Road, Suite 100
Lincoln, NE 68512
www.iuniverse.com

ISBN: 0-595-26735-1

Printed in the United States of America

To my son, John-Daniel Kelley, who taught me to see animals in a different way.

Contents

Introduction ix

CHAPTER 1 The First Dogs to Ride a Rocket—August 15,
1951 1

CHAPTER 2 Animals Go Into Space 9

CHAPTER 3 The Dog Astronaut Program Begins 15

CHAPTER 4 Training Dogs to Fly on Rockets 21

CHAPTER 5 Smelaya's Flight 29

CHAPTER 6 Dogs Go Higher 37

CHAPTER 7 Laika, Space Heroine 47

CHAPTER 8 Satellite Dogs 57

CHAPTER 9 Space Dogs Finish Their Work 73

Epilogue November 1997 81

Flight Log A record of those who flew 83

Glossary 85

Bibliography 89

Introduction

Before the international space station, before probes visited the other planets in our solar system, before humans first orbited the earth in space capsules, animals were shot into space aboard rockets. Some made high-altitude flights into the upper layers of the atmosphere. Others flew beyond the atmosphere to circle the earth. These animals faced all of the unknown dangers in the early years of rocket travel. They taught scientists what they needed to know to send humans into space.

Two countries participated in the early development of space travel—the United States and the Soviet Union (now Russia). Although the American space program used monkeys and chimpanzees as their animal astronauts, the Soviet Union used dogs. Dozens of dogs became astronauts. They rode in rockets and actually flew in space, long before humans did. That's what makes them the pioneers of space travel. Because they did things and went places no person had ever gone. Their experiences allowed the Soviet Union to achieve many of the biggest accomplishments in the early development of space travel. They got ahead of the United States in the race into space.

Eventually, humans would take over the role of astronauts from animals. But for 15 years Space Dogs had the attention of the world as they rode rockets into space. The age of the space dogs extended from the first launch in 1951, until the final, record-breaking, 22-day dog flight in 1966. Some of dogs died in the name of science, some became famous. They were all pioneers of space travel. This is their story.

Although *Space Dogs* dramatizes events of the space dog program, this is an accurate, historical account of this little-known chapter in the history of the exploration of space.

1

The First Dogs to Ride a Rocket—August 15, 1951

In darkness an automobile pulled to a stop outside the launch bunker at the Soviet rocket facility at Kapustin Yar, near the Caspian Sea. Its headlights illuminated a line of parked cars and men standing beside them. Anatoly Blagon stepped from the car and greeted the engineers, doctors, and other scientists who had gathered for this important event. Blagon removed his hat and wiped his forehead with a handkerchief. Kapustin Yar was located in the southernmost part of Russia where summers got hot and dry. Even before sunrise, the temperature had reached 80 degrees. Blagon, a thin man, seemed to wilt in the heat. He headed the government committee overseeing the current rocket experiments.

He walked from man to man, asking about their work, wanting the latest information. Years of effort had gone into today's launch. So much depended on it. These men had designed the rocket and the container, or capsule, that would carry the passengers. They had test fired many rockets, fixing and improving them. All of that work led up to the rocket that now sat on the launch pad some distance away.

These men had also trained the crew that would fly aboard that rocket. Several hours ago the astronauts had been placed in a capsule the size of a small suitcase in the nose of the rocket. Their names were Tsygan (which means Gypsy in Russian) and Dezik. They were dogs, and now they waited, as the men waited, to make history. They were about to become the first dogs ever to fly in a rocket.

Why were dogs being used as the first astronauts? Early rockets were not strong enough to lift anything as heavy as a human being. And there were too many unknown dangers. Scientists had visions of humans flying in space and visiting other planets. But first they had to build bigger and better rockets. So, dogs were selected to be the astronauts of the Soviet rocket program. Nine dogs had gone into training months earlier to prepare for this flight and the other flights that would follow.

For several years, the United States had been launching its animal astronauts (monkeys) into the upper atmosphere. Five monkeys launched and five monkeys died. Rocket travel was a complicated and dangerous business. No one had yet launched any animal in a rocket and recovered it alive. If the Soviets were successful today, they would beat the Americans.

The launch security officer appeared before the men at the cars, his figure lit by the harsh outside lights on the launch bunker. How very glad he was to have such important guests on this important occasion, he said. "For those of you who have never before seen a launch, I know you will find it very exciting." His own voice sounded excited, but he paused, then continued in a more serious tone. "However, for your own safety and so that our staff can do their job efficiently, I must request that you remain by your vehicles, both during the launch and during the recovery of the animals." He heard mumbled sounds of agreement.

The red glow of a new day lay on the horizon. It was time. Launches lifted off just minutes before sunrise. That way the rising sun would light up the rocket as it climbed, making it easier to follow from the ground. As the moment of launch approached, the scientists stood in a line staring towards the launch pad. Silence settled over the scene. The scientists and the rocket waited beneath a canopy of bright stars, where some day they hoped to travel.

First came the brilliant flash of light as giant flames burst from the rocket engines. Then "Whooomp," the tremendous roar of the engines, like an explosion, reached their ears and pushed against their bodies like unseen hands. It seemed to rob the very air from their lungs. All of the men stood with mouths open, heads tilting back, as they followed the rocket, climbing through the night sky. The morning sun, peaking over the horizon, painted the rocket with reddish light. Up, up, until it climbed out of sight.

These cramped conditions are typical of the capsules used on the early flights. Here Damka (left) and Kozyavka are being loaded into a rocket. *Novosti (London).*

Now came the hard part—the waiting. If things went according to plan, the rocket engine would burn for several minutes, thrusting the rocket to a speed of 2,600 miles per hour and lifting it 63 miles into the air. Blagon checked his watch. In the next few minutes, he could predict where the rocket should be. It would quickly climb through the bottom layer of the atmosphere, the layer of air where we live and where weather happens.

He watched the second hand sweep around his watch. Now, it would be about 25 miles high, passing through the stratosphere, where the air begins to thin out and there is not enough oxygen to breath. The second hand circled his watch again. "Right…now," he thought, it would be 40 miles high, entering the mesosphere, where temperatures fell as low as -173 degrees, and shooting stars streak the darkness.

Blagon turned his gaze overhead. The sun lit a line of clouds in the eastern sky. At just about that moment, the rocket would be climbing above 50 miles high, entering the "upper atmosphere," the very edge of space. No blanket of air offered protection at that altitude. There rays from the sun could heat objects to several hundred degrees. He took a deep breath. What a great and dangerous adventure for the dogs, he thought.

At that point, the capsule containing the dogs was supposed to separate from the main rocket and fall back towards earth. The parachute could not open that high up; there was not enough air for it to work. The capsule would fall, down and down, going faster and faster, for nearly 60 miles. When it reached four miles above the ground, the parachute was supposed to open and float the dogs safely to earth. That is how things were *supposed* to work. Things did not always work the way they were supposed to. There had been accidents on some of the earlier rocket launches. Many things could go wrong. With the rocket now out of sight, no one knew for sure what was really happening.

The scientists waited through the painful minutes for some sign of the rocket's return. Blagon had not moved a muscle since the last time he checked his watch. He pulled himself out of the trance and wiped his face with a handkerchief. So much depended on what happened in the next few minutes. Tomorrow he would have to make a report about this launch to government officials. A failure here could mean the end of the space dog program. Or, the very least, it would result in a long delay. It would give the Americans time to finally launch their monkey astronaut successfully. Ten minutes went by. He began to pace. His thoughts twisted together with worry. Did the rocket work properly? Had it stayed on course? Eleven minutes. Did the dogs survive the incredible forces of acceleration? Did the capsule separate from the rocket properly? Twelve minutes. He sat on the bumper of his car, suddenly very tired.

"Vot eto!" Someone yelled, and Blagon jumped to his feet. "There it is!" All eyes followed where the man pointed. They saw a long dark object falling rapidly through grey sky a few miles away. Blagon felt a tightening around his heart. "No parachute," he thought. A bright flash of light indicated where the object smashed into the ground. Then shortly the rumbling sound of an explosion reached the observers like distant thunder. A few of the men clamped a hand over their mouths to hold in a cry, horrified that something had gone terribly wrong. But others hastened to explain that it had just been the rocket's main body falling down and the remains of its fuel exploding.

More anxious minutes passed before a call went out again. "It's coming down." All heads turned at once to look. A small cloud seemed to have blossomed in the sky. It picked up pink rays of light from the sunrise. It was the parachute, slowly lowering the nose cone of the rocket, which contained the dog capsule.

The men exploded into action. Forgetting their instructions to remain where they were, they rushed to their cars and sped off across the open ground, kicking up clouds of dust. Blagon took the lead, his heart racing, his foot heavy on the gas pedal. Flat plains surrounded Kapustin Yar for miles. The line of cars sped across them, lined up like a flock of geese, turning this way and that to follow the descending parachute. They converged on the spot where the capsule had touched down, jumped from their cars and crowded around, waiting anxiously to learn the fate of the dogs. The capsule must have hit the ground hard, because part of the metal side had dented.

"Stand back. Give them room to work," people said when the recovery crew arrived. The crew fumbled screw drivers out of their toolbox and began removing the plate that covered the capsule. Blagon leaned over the men. The instant the plate came off, he could see one of the dogs—black gleaming eyes in a face of white fur, that seemed to look up at him with surprise. "They're ok," he yelled.

This "staged landing" demonstrates how the dogs and recording instruments were recovered from the nose cone of the rocket once it had returned to earth. Pictured here are Kozyavka (left) and Damka.
Novosti (London).

The dogs were unstrapped from their harnesses and slipped from the tight space of their capsule. It was hard to tell who was more excited, the dogs or the scientists. Tsygan and Dezik danced around from man to man, yipping and accepting the enthusiastic petting from everyone. Their tails fluttered with happiness. Tsygan put her front paws on Blagon's leg. She was the white faced dog he'd seen in the rocket. He picked her up and gave her a hug. She licked his face, and he laughed. That was as curious a sight as anything on this historic day. No one had ever seen Blagon laugh before.

The recovery crew gave the dogs a quick examination. Dezik was in fine shape, but Tsygan had a scrape on her belly. When the capsule hit ground and the metal crumpled, it had pushed in and bruised her. She would need a little time to recover, but she would be just fine. Dezik and Tsygan had played their role in space flight history by being the first animals to survive a ride in a rocket.

Dezik would fly on another rocket the following week, with a dog named Lisa. But disaster would strike that flight when the parachute failed to open. Both dogs died when their capsule crashed to the ground. When Blagon learned of the accident, he immediately drove back to Kapustin Yar and announced that Tsygan would not be flying on any more rockets. He took her home with him to Moscow to be his pet. Tsygan lived to a ripe old age. In later years Blagon and Tsygan would often be seen walking the streets of Moscow, clearly the best of friends.

2

Animals Go Into Space

Why were the United States and the Soviet Union shooting animals up in rockets?

Space travel seems so common to us now—landings on the Moon, probes to Mars, frequent launchings of the space shuttle—that it's hard to realize that some 50 years ago, it was all very new and unknown. The first big rocket (the V-2) capable of going high in the atmosphere, had been developed as a weapon by Germany during World War II. After the defeat of Germany, both the United States and the Soviet Union captured German rocket equipment and used German scientists to begin their own rocket programs. Beginning in the late 1940s, the competition was very fierce between the two countries. Each wanted to be the first to develop bigger and better rockets that took them closer to space.

From the start the ultimate goal of both programs was to achieve space travel by humans. But so little was known about space or about flying in a rocket. How do you make a rocket big enough to go into into space? Could humans travel in a rocket? Could they survive in space? What type of equipment would be needed to keep them safe in space? How did you bring them safely back to earth? Everything was new. Everything had to be invented and tried out for the first time. So many problems had to be solved.

One of the many questions facing scientists involved how the human body would hold up to rocket travel. V-2 rockets sped along at about 2,500 mph. To break free of earth's gravity and reach orbit, a rocket must travel at least 25,000 mph. As a rocket accelerates to those incredible speeds, the force of gravity is magnified. It's the same force that pushes you back in your seat when your car speeds up quickly. It is called "g force," g standing for "gravity." A 175 pound astronaut riding aboard a V-2 rocket would experience about 4 g's, or four times the weight of gravity. It would be as though he weighed 700 pounds. Could a person move or breath under such a force? Would the heart still be able to pump blood? No one knew.

In space, the opposite effect is encountered—weightlessness or zero gravity. People or objects literally float in air. There is no "up" or "down," no floor or ceiling. Could a person live without gravity? Would their organs work? Would they be able to think? Would they be able to perform simple tasks? No one knew.

Space itself offered its own hazards, such as radiation and micro meteorites speeding along as fast as bullets. Then, there was the challenge of simply living in a tiny capsule circling in space. Could people function in such cramped conditions for long periods of time? How would they eat or go to the bathroom? All of these problems had to be investigated and solved before a human could risk a trip into space.

Animals were chosen to lead the way for humans. Animals became the test subjects for space travel. In laboratory experiments and high-altitude balloons, in suborbital flights that flew high into the atmosphere and fell back to earth, and orbital flights that went into space and circled around the earth, animals were used to measure the effects of space travel. Of course, dogs were not the only test animals. A large variety of animals earned their wings to advance our knowledge of space flight. Invertebrates (animals without backbones), such as insects, jellyfish, and even one-celled animals like the amoeba, flew on many rocket flights in those early years. From these animals scientists learned how rocket flight affected them, how organisms developed in weightlessness, and how their genes were affected by radiation. The other type of animals used were vertebrates (animals with backbones), such as fish, frogs, turtles, mice, rats, rabbits, dogs, cats, monkeys, and chimpanzees. They too earned their astronaut wings aboard early rocket flights. Because vertebrates are a lot more like humans, scientists could learn how space affected their bodies and behavior and then compare it to human bodies and behavior.

Many countries have honored animal astronauts on postage stamps. These, from the country of Niger, show the chimpanzee named Ham, who flew on a suborbital flight for the U.S. in 1961; the dog Laika, the first living creature to orbit the earth; Felix the cat, who rode a French rocket to 120 miles in 1963, and a spider, who represents all of the nameless insects and other living creatures who rode on rockets.

Many animals served in the space programs of the United States, the Soviet Union, and other countries, as well. Some animals, especially mice, continue to serve to this day. But for a few years in the 1950s and

1960s, the most famous animal astronauts in the world were the space dogs of the Soviet Union.

The early accomplishments of both countries led the way to the development of human space flight. Here are a few of the "first steps" that led from then to now.

Dates in Early Space Flight History

June 11, 1948—First suborbital flight by an animal

A rhesus monkey named Albert flew to an altitude of 37 miles but died when his parachute failed to open. This was the first of six animal flights launched by the United States between 1948 and 1951. Five monkeys and several mice died before the first successful flight.

August 15, 1951—First suborbital flight in which the animals survived

The Soviet Union launched the dogs, Dezik and Tsygan, to an altitude of 63 miles and recovered them successfully.

September 20, 1951—First U.S. suborbital flight in which the animals lived

A Rhesus monkey named Yorick, along with 11 mice, flew in a rocket to an altitude of 44 miles and returned safely.

October 4, 1957—First artificial earth satellite

The Soviet Union launched Sputnik 1, the first man-made object to orbit the earth.

November 3, 1957—First animal orbital flight

The Soviet space dog Laika, orbited the earth for four days before dying in space.

January 31, 1958—First U.S. satellite launched, Explorer I

August 19, 1960—First animals to be recovered successfully from orbit

The Soviet Union recovered the dogs Belka and Strelka from orbit.

April 12, 1961—First human orbital flight

Soviet astronaut Yuri Gagarin orbited the earth.

May 5, 1961—First human suborbital flight

U.S. astronaut Alan Shepard became the first human to make a suborbital rocket flight. The Soviet Union had decided not to use humans in suborbital flights.

November 29, 1961—First U.S. animal orbital flight

Enos the chimpanzee was recovered successfully from orbit.

February 20, 1962—First U.S. human orbital flight

John Glenn completed a successful orbital flight.

3

The Dog Astronaut Program Begins

Spring 1951. Two men drove their car slowly along the back allleys of Moscow. They watched carefully for movement among the piles of trash they passed. Night was approaching, but they still had more work to do.

"There." One of the men pointed, and the driver jerked to a stop. They eased open the car doors. When you were a hunter, you stepped slowly and softly. They peered into the shadows. Sometimes when they explored an alley, they found only a cat or a rat. They had found pigs, a mule, a goat. The city teemed with wildlife. The driver wore thick glasses that always slipped down his nose. He had to tilt his head back to see down the alley. "Aaah," he whispered, as the animal stepped into full view. This time they were lucky; they had found what they were looking for—a dog.

"You're a sorry looking mutt," the driver said in a soothing tone. Only a little larger than a house cat, the dog was of no particular breed. It had a lean and hungry look, like all of the other strays that made their home on the streets of Moscow. It was, in fact, exactly the kind of dog they had been looking for.

The men shook meat scraps out of a newspaper onto the ground. These mongrels were always wary, but they were always hungry too. They studied this one carefully to see how it would react. They did not want mean dogs or nervous dogs. This one wagged its tail and marched right up to them. "Oh, ho, very brave," the driver said. One of the dog's ears poked straight up and the other drooped on its side, making it look lopsided. The men glanced at each other and nodded. They scooped up the dog, placed it in the cage in the back seat of their car, and drove away.

These men were not dog catchers, they were scientists with the Soviet rocket program, and they were recruiting the animals that would be trained to fly on rockets and travel in space. Unlike the United States, which had chosen to use monkeys as its animal astronauts, the Soviet Union thought dogs would make better space travelers. Dogs would be calmer, they thought, and better able to deal with the stress than other animals. They felt that monkeys were too nervous and frail, and too subject to disease.

Soviet scientists had already determined from earlier experiments that the best type of dog was a mongrel, the tough little dogs that ran wild in most villages and cities in the Soviet Union. These dogs had experienced hardship, had known hunger and cold. They would hold up better to the hard training and the rigorous conditions of rocket travel. Therefore, when the Soviet space program wanted to recruit its first class of space dogs, it sent scientists to the Soviet capital, Moscow. They rounded up strays from the streets and got other mongrel dogs donated by their owners. The dogs would be helping the cause of science, they were told, and so the owners agreed.

When the two men returned from their hunting expedition in the alleys of Moscow, they delivered the dog with the droopy ear to the medical unit of the rocket program. The man with the thick glasses said, "You're going into outer space, little one. It's a great honor." They stood droopy ear on a table, and men in white coats looked her over.

Dogs were being selected for the first group of animal astronauts that would fly on the six rocket launches planned for the fall and winter of 1951. Some would remain in training for other flights in the years to come. But the selection process was not so easy. The space program required a very particular type of dog.

First, these canine astronauts had to be small, 13 to 16 pounds. The early rockets were not powerful enough to lift heavy loads, and they had very little room for passengers. Next, the dogs had to be hearty to withstand the conditions of rocket flight. Ideally, they should also be female and have light-colored fur. Being female was important because the space suit the dogs would wear had a device that let them go to the toilet, but it was designed to work only with females. Light fur was necessary because movies were made of the dogs in flight. The camera could see a light-colored dog better in the dark capsule. The age of the dog was also a factor. Dogs under 1 ½ years of age were too nervous, and those over six were considered too old.

Because it was often difficult to find dogs that met all of these criteria, scientists were delighted when they found a new candidate. Sometimes, when they had a good candidate who didn't have all these qualities, they tried to force the issue. Once they had a dog in training named T'ma (Darkness), who was well qualified but had black fur. So, they tried to bleach it white with hydrogen peroxide. The bleach was applied in small square test patches. Unfortunately, the fur turned red instead of white. For months, poor T'ma walked around looking like a checkerboard, with red squares on her back and sides.

T'ma was one of the many dogs who went through training but never flew on a rocket. Those dogs also played an important role in the research preparing dogs to fly. In the laboratory, scientists were able to study their reaction to some conditions of rocket travel. This helped them to better design the equipment that would be needed by the dogs that did fly.

Droopy ear had a few things working in her favor. She was a female and had honey brown fur. She weighed in at 14 ½ pounds and was judged to be about 2 years old. She met the first requirements. But that did not mean that she automatically became a dog astronaut. She would have to go through a few tests first. Only if she earned grades of "good" or "excellent" would she join the elite ranks of the space dogs.

When the dogs had made it this far in the evaluation process, they were given a name. What would they call old droopy ear? Sometimes an obvious name suggested itself. One dog had been given the name Albina, which is Russian for "Whitie." A later dog with white fur was named Snezhinka "Snow Flake." A dog who entered the program later, when dark-furred dogs could be used, got the name Chernushka "Blackie" and another was named Ugolek, "Little piece of coal." Others were given whatever name their handler could think of. The most famous human astronaut in the Soviet space program was Yuri Gagarin, the first human to orbit the earth. He attended the launch of the dog that made the last flight before his own. Her flight would test some of the very equipment that he would use when launched into orbit. He named her Zvezdochka "Little Star."

Droopy ear had impressed her handlers with how fearlessly she walked up to humans and other dogs. Each new person or animal entering the room had to be investigated. Would this human give her a pat on the head; would this dog greet her with a friendly sniff or a growl? This fearlessness earned her the name Smelaya, which was Russian for "Brave One."

She would need to be brave for what she was about to face. As the selection process continued, dogs were introduced to some of the equipment that would be used in their training. The following day, they dressed Smelaya in tight clothing, crammed her into a tiny capsule on the end of large mechanical arm, and spun her in circles at great speeds. This is how it would feel to fly in a rocket. If a dog couldn't stand the experience, it wasn't astronaut material. Some dogs squirmed, barked, and chewed at their container. They were removed from training. Some dogs became depressed and would not eat. They were let go, too. But some of the dogs adjusted to this strange experience. They would be the ones who could accept the training, even if they didn't like it.

Smelaya performed well. A few weeks after she had been brought in as a stray off the streets, Smelaya became one of nine dogs who made up the original group of Space Dogs. The other dogs in her training class were: Albina, Bobik, Dezik, Kozyavka, Ryzhik, Lisa, Malyshka, and Tsygan. As time went by, other dogs would be added or dismissed from training.

Now, only one step remained to prepare the dogs for training. They had to be separated into different groups, based upon their personalities. It was an important decision. Handlers and veterinarians had carefully watched their behavior since they had arrived. Some dogs were frisky, some nervous, some were cooperative, some slow moving. Different types of rocket flights required dogs with different personalities. For instance, a nervous dog would not do well in a long, orbital flight which would require her to stay in a tiny capsule for a day or more.

The even-tempered dogs went into one group, restless ones into another, and sluggish ones into a third group. Active and continually curious, Smelaya landed with the restless dogs. This meant that she would probably fly on one of the shorter, suborbital flights—one of the flights that would be launched that fall.

4

Training Dogs to Fly on Rockets

Smelaya and the other dogs lived in a fenced in kennel at the launch site, tended carefully by handlers and veterinarians. The area had grass, trees, and flowers where the dogs could romp. Each dog had her own cage. A hand-painted sign on every door gave the dog's name. They received twice-daily exercise walks, a nutritional diet, and regular physical examinations.

Smelaya soon became a favorite of the handlers. When they came to feed her, she liked to scoot from her cage and frolic around the kennel, stirring up the other dogs, making them yip and bark in unison. When she took her exercise walks, she ran circles around her handlers.

You would hear them yelling, "Smelaya, come back here!" Sometimes she listened to them and sometimes she did not. Certainly not when she was having so much fun.

But Smelaya's life was about to take a new direction. From this point she would enter into the intense training that would prepare her for a rocket flight, her moment in space history. Her work as an animal astronaut was about to begin.

Those early days of her training began like this: First she would be dressed in a restraining suit, which was a knit vest and short pants of a light silk cloth with rings attached. She would always stand up, give herself a good shake, then accept the unfamiliar feel of being clothed. Then it was off to a training room to spend time in a "confinement capsule."

An eerie feeling crept over anyone when they first entered the confinement capsule room. An instant chorus of barking and whimpering greeted them, from many unseen dogs. A variety of chambers and compartments crowded the room. Some lined the walls, some stood high on metal legs, looking like strange beasts. Wire mesh covered the side of some capsules, through which a visitor might glimpse a gleaming eye or a moist nose. Other capsules had only a tiny window connecting to the outside world.

All of the dogs began their astronaut training in confinement capsules. They had to be taught to overcome their fear of the conditions they would experience while riding a rocket. Basically, rockets were very cramped, very noisy, very fast, and vibrated a lot. And when that scary ride was over, the dog had to parachute back to earth from 60 miles up, through air so thin you couldn't breath it and so cold you could freeze in the blink of an eye.

Smelaya growled when taken to the capsule. She had been here before and didn't like it. Still, at the urging of the handler, she allowed herself to be tucked into the tiny space. Chains clipped onto the rings of her restraining suit, attached her to the capsule walls from four sides. This allowed virtually no movement. The door was shut on her for one hour. In the days to come, she would be required to stay there for two hours, then four hours, and finally for several days. It was not a pleasant experience for a dog. They enjoy the company of other dogs and humans. Smelaya showed her displeasure by barking and scratching at the capsule.

It might seem cruel to someone watching, but it was the very first thing that a space dog had to learn—how to be alone, in a very small space, for a long time. Even on rocket flights that lasted only 30 minutes, the dog would be loaded into the capsule several hours before the launch. They had to remain calm that whole time.

The famous space dog Veterok would sometimes become so nervous during this exercise that he would "lose control" and squirm about continuously. Nothing anyone said or did would calm him. But that nervous outburst gave no indication that Veterok would later become famous for his record-breaking orbital flight of 22 days, made along with his companion Ugolek.

Training in the confinement capsule eventually made Veterok comfortable with the tiny space available inside a rocket. The more familiar a dog was with what it would be like to ride a rocket, the more likely she would be able to handle the stress. So, training equipment was designed to show a dog what it would be like inside the capsule, and what it would feel and sound like during the launch of a rocket, the re-entry of the rocket through the atmosphere, the landing back on earth, and finally, what it would be like in space.

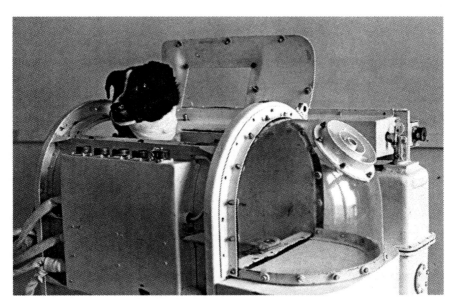

Veterok about to enter a laboratory test chamber. Test chambers were used to introduce the dogs to isolation and different air pressures. *Novosti (London).*

Other unusual experiences awaited the dogs on a rocket ride, and they also had to be introduced to them in their training. One, was having *extra gravity* during part of the flight, and having *no gravity* during another part of the flight. When these rockets sped up from 0 to 3,000 miles per hour, a dog would be pressed down with a weight that was four or five times what they weighed on earth. They would experience 4 or 5 times the weight of gravity, that is 4 or 5 G's. Faster rockets caused even higher G's.

When the rocket, climbing through the atmosphere, had used up all of its fuel and finished accelerating, it would continue to coast for a while, until it reached its peak altitude. It was during this coasting phase of the flight that the dogs experienced no gravity, which is called "weightlessness." During later flights, when the dogs actually circled the earth in space, weightlessness continued all during their orbits, for hours or days. During these early rocket flights, however, the dogs would experience only a few minutes of weightlessness.

A machine called a centrifuge can create the G-forces of a speeding rocket by spinning a capsule around in a circle. It works like a twirling amusement park ride that presses its rider harder and harder against the outside wall the faster it spins. When they brought Smelaya in for her first ride, they strapped her tightly onto the couch of the centrifuge capsule. Her keen eyes followed every movement as workers hooked electrical wires to her and flipped switches on and off. These would record her breathing and heart rate. A movie camera in the capsule would record her reactions.

The door closed, the motor started, and the capsule–at the end of a long metal arm–began to spin. "Two...three...three and one half." The worker controlling the machine read off numbers as the speed increased. These were the G forces climbing. The movie camera showed Smelaya head flopping back and forth. It was suddenly three times heavier than it had been, and she struggled to control the weight. "Four...five...six." The machine spun faster, increasing the force pushing down on Smelaya. Finally, the powerful g-force pressed her body tightly against the outside wall of the capsule. Her heart rate and breathing increased slightly. She was fine, though surely confused. This was exactly what it would feel like when she rode a rocket.

Smelaya was groggy after her first ride, as though she couldn't quite wake up from a deep sleep. The man with the thick glasses was the one to lift her gently from the capsule, carry her back to the kennel, and lay her in the cage. Veterinarians watched her closely. The most important part of the centrifuge ride was how the dogs behaved after their ride. How confused were they? How long did it take them to recover? In a short while Smelaya was moving and looking more alert. After several more rides, it hardly seemed to bother her at all. Back from a ride, she immediately stood up, curious about happenings in the kennel. High marks for Smelaya!

Creating the experience of weightlessness was harder to do. It required the dogs to take a ride in a high-altitude airplane. This not only introduced them to the feeling of flying, but brief periods of weightlessness could be created. The dogs could float like a feather in air, with no weight of gravity pulling them down. Several dogs at a time would be taken up. For less than a minute they floated in the air, light as a dandelion seed on the wind.

Each day another round of training took place. The kennel and the laboratories buzzed with activity. Some dogs might be getting their exercise in the fenced enclosure, others might be spending a day resting in their cages. Here you would see a dog trotting down a hallway behind her favorite handler on the way to the centrifuge or the vibration test. In another room, one would be getting a bath with baby soap (the only soap used on the dogs' sensitive skin), while another was being taught to eat like an astronaut. Even eating and drinking were no easy task for a space dog. In the weightlessness of space, water and food would float around the capsule. A special jelly-like food was created that stuck to the sides of a food container. Like all of the other strange experiences of rocket travel, the dogs had to be trained to eat this unusual food.

More than a month into her training, the man with the thick glasses fetched Smelaya from her cage. He petted her more than usual as he took her to a separate building. He knew this would be a hard day for her. In that training room, a thick post protruded from the floor, supporting a metal platform with a padded cradle. This was the vibration machine, the hardest test for the dogs.

When a rocket takes off, the thrust of its engines makes it vibrate very strongly. At the same time, the engines roar with incredible power and noise. Any passenger aboard the rocket, has the double discomfort of being shaken about and deafened by the thunder of the engines. If the dogs weren't familiar with this experience, they would panic when they took their first rocket ride.

The man with the thick glasses had seen the vibration machine work. Its vibrations did not seem all that strong. If you placed your hand on the metal platform, it only giggled the skin of your arm. But if you left it there awhile, you started to feel a deeper shaking. The movement sank deep into your muscles, then to your very bones. And you thought you would be shaken to pieces. The machine was also very loud, making a "clunk, clunk, clunk" noise as the post shook the table. The handlers in the room could not speak to each other above the noise when it was operating.

The man strapped Smelaya into the cradle, then attached the wires that would measure heart rate, breathing, and blood pressure. She was Smelaya, the Brave One, and she took all this fuss with great calm. When the machine was turned on, the vibration did not seem so bad, and the knocking noise was just beginning to get loud. Smelaya's droopy ear stood up; she seemed perky and alert to this strange experience.

But as the vibrations got stronger, everything changed. Smelaya began to strain at the harness holding her in place. She wanted to get off this machine, away from this noise. A look of terror came into her eyes. She had always stood on solid ground, but now the earth shook beneath her. The noise grew so loud that it felt like a solid sharp object stabbing into the brain.

The man with the thick glasses stroked Smelaya's head. It seemed to quiet her a little, but fear stayed in her eyes. They froze with a straight-ahead gaze. Her blood pressure and heart beat increased. At first her breathing nearly stopped, as though she was too scared to even thinking about taking a breath. Then a gulp of air, and her chest moved in and out.

When the machine was turned off, and Smelaya taken from the cradle, she gave no reaction to the man and his petting. In fact, she fell asleep in his arms. That was a typical reaction. The wires, still reading her body signs, showed that they had already returned to normal. Sleep was her body's way of recovering from the shock.

◆   ◆   ◆

June had arrived, and the pace of training activity began to speed up. New dogs appeared in the kennel, their names printed in black letters on their cage doors: Chizhik, Mishka, Neputevyy. Bold Smelaya introduced herself to all of them.

Training schedules were getting crowded. Every other day, when Smelaya went back to the vibration table, another dog would just be finishing her shaky ride. Off she would go in the arms of her handler, while Smelaya got strapped in place. As with the other stressful things that she had to learn, she began to adapt to this one as well. Gradually, she began to accept the vibration and continuous noise more calmly and without the paralyzing fear that gripped her the first time. Every other day she went through the test again, each time spending a little more time on the machine.

One sunny day in late June the man with the thick glasses led Smelaya outside to a small yard and made her sit down. Then out came Kozyavka, who sat three feet away. Then Bobik and Albina appeared and finally all of the original nine dogs. The veterinarians stood in front of them, looking and writing notes on their clip boards, looking again and talking. In the strange world of the space dogs, even sitting still was a test. Space dogs had to be very patient.

But this occasion was more than a sitting-still contest. The date for the launch of the first dog rocket was fast approaching, and its crew had to be selected. Two dogs would fly in the rocket, but which two? Having all the dogs together gave everyone a chance to look them over, to compare. Some small bit of behavior, some quality overlooked in training, might help the trainers decide.

The man with the thick glass flapped his hands at Smelaya, urging her to sit up straight. That wouldn't affect the decision, but he still wanted her to look her best. He felt as nervous as a parent watching his daughter at a beauty contest. How proud he would be if Smelaya was chosen to go first. But, Smelaya got her signals crossed. Instead of sitting up straight, she let out a bark and a howl. All the people, and the dogs too, looked in her direction, unsure what to do.

"Shhh." The man held a finger to his lips and tried to quiet her. This was not good. This was not good at all. Soon the veterinarians surrounded her, some talking to her, some motioning with their hands for her to stop, some writing on their clipboards. But Smelaya kept barking.

Kozyavka began to answer back. Then Albina started too, then Bobik. The other handlers tried to quiet their dogs. But, soon all of the dogs had taken Smelaya's suggestion and blended their voices together. The man with the thick glasses could not miss the annoyed expressions on the faces of the veterinarians. It was not good for a space dog to get out of control. Forget any thought of getting on the first rocket. Now he just wondered if they would let her stay in the program.

5

Smelaya's Flight

"Smelaya?" The man with the thick glasses came early one morning. "Smelaya. Are you awake?" He rattled the door of her cage.

She got up, stretched herself thoroughly, front legs and body, then back legs to their full extension. Then she came to greet him. "You have been selected to go on the fourth flight. I was just at the meeting where they decided." He stuck his fingers through the wire to pet her nose. "They said you were a brave dog, and very strong." He smiled at this play of words on her name, Smelaya—Brave One—as the brave one licked his fingers. "You will be famous, Smelaya. Your name will be written in the stars."

He opened her cage door and Smelaya jumped to the ground. He led her down the path that ran through the kennel. The other dogs began to stir. Dezik whimpered, Kozyavka barked, Bobik waited wide eyed for her breakfast. They stopped before a cage marked with the name "Ryzhik." "Here is your traveling companion." He lifted Ryzhik from her cage and put her on the ground. Ryzhik was a long-haired white dog, with grey spots, who always looked a bit rumpled, as though her fur had been brushed the wrong way. The two dogs gave each other a courteous sniff.

It was the summer of 1951, the historic summer of 1951, the summer when dogs were flying in rockets. Only last week, Tsygan and Dezik had become the first dogs to ride a rocket. Now five more launches would follow quickly. Five launches in five weeks. Everything had to be in order. Everything had to run smoothly.

All of these launches would carry two dogs. Having two dogs onboard allowed scientists to compare results. If one dog reacted in a certain way, they could compare her behavior with that of the other dog. If one dog panicked in the tightness of the capsule, was it just her personality or a reaction that all dogs would have? If one dog had a problem breathing, was it just her or a problem in the equipment?

Smelaya and Ryzhik trotted off behind the man with the thick glasses. As usual Smelaya ran far and wide, while Ryzhik marched along like a soldier on parade. The man stopped, as he always did on such exercise walks, to stare off in the distance where a new rocket sat on the launch pad. The R-1 rocket being used for the dog flights was an impressive machine. Standing on the launchpad, it looked like a narrow building, 5 ½ feet wide and over 55 feet high. On top of the large tail fins, sat the main body that held the fuel tanks, and above that rose the pointy nose section that contained the dog capsule. The second launch was scheduled for tomorrow, carrying the dogs Lisa and Dezik. The following week Mishka and Chizhik would fly. "And then," the man gestured dramatically with his finger.

He looked down at the two little dogs in his care—Ryzhik, standing by his feet, and old droopy ear, pushing through the bushes along the path. "Smelaya!" he yelled, to remind her where she belonged. She took her time coming back to him. He knelt beside the dogs and ruffled the thick fur on their necks. Then he pointed to the rocket. "In about two weeks," he said, "Cosmonaut Ryzhik and the Great Smelaya will sit atop that powerful rocket and take the ride of their lives, up to the edge of space. And I will be very, very proud."

◆   ◆   ◆

Work began especially early the next day, July 29th. The man with the thick glasses arrived before dawn and joined others who had gathered in the observation area. The last of the fuel trucks was just pulling away from the launch pad. They had filled the rocket with liquid oxygen, alcohol, and hydrogen peroxide, the fuels burned by its mighty engine. Wisps of vapor from the frigid liquid oxygen escaped from the sides of the rocket, like smoke from a smoldering fire.

It was the day for the launch of the second dog flight. Canine astronauts Lisa and Dezik had been sealed inside the rocket several hours ago. Now, a slice of day light on the horizon signaled time for launch.

The flash of the engines announced the liftoff. All of the men, in unison, brought their fingers to their ears to guard against the incredible roar that followed seconds later. The bright flames from the rocket glowed like a star in the twilight, hurting their eyes. The captain of the recovery team had warned them in the strongest terms to remain where they were and not to go chasing after the rocket when it returned, as they had done last time. However, the man with the thick glasses had heard some of the others saying that they would ignore that advice and again race their cars to the landing site. There was still so much excitement in the launches. Everyone wanted to see for themselves the dogs the moment they stepped from the capsule, like aliens landing from another planet. It was as though people still couldn't believe that all of this was really happening, that dogs were actually flying in rockets.

The rocket climbed its fiery path into the heavens, until the last pinpoint of flame disappeared. Then came the painful waiting. Some men paced, some sat in their cars, ready to speed away as soon as they saw where the capsule would land. Shortly, someone shouted when he spotted the rocket body falling through the grey sky to crash with an explosion. Everyone scanned the sky for the white puff of parachute bringing the dogs home. A car engine was turned on.

All those watching eyes saw it at the same time, not a parachute but another grey chunk of the rocket—the payload section containing the dog capsule. It sliced through the sky—no white parachute above it to control its fall, to slow it down—and crashed on the ground. The man with the thick glasses gasped, the only person to make a sound. He had known those small dogs, petted them, played with them, trained them. Everyone else was too stunned to speak or move. None of the cars pulled away. Instead the men watched as the recovery team climbed into their truck and drove across the empty landscape towards the crash site.

The loss of the two dogs, Lisa and Dezik, changed everyone's mood. From giddy excitement to a somber awareness of the task before them. The instruments recovered from that crash site, revealed that the dogs had done well during the flight, but the vibration of the rocket during launch had broken the switch that should have opened the parachute. It was a reminder for everyone that this was a dangerous business, where things could and did go wrong. "Accidents were to be expected," some said. That was why the scientists had to iron out all of the problems before humans rode the rockets. It was why dogs rode the rockets for now.

The third launch was postponed for two weeks. Everyone worked more intently. Things needed to be fixed and improved. All the parts of the rocket had to be checked and rechecked and checked again. To the man with the thick glasses, even the dogs seemed on edge. They didn't eat as well and didn't do as well in training. But everyone worked with more of a purpose now, because they didn't want another accident.

Finally, on August 15 they were ready for the next launch. The launch went smoothly, but the waiting was more painful. They stood in a line, peering intently at the grey sky. First the rocket body came down. And then…there it was! The parachute. White and glorious in the morning sun, bringing Mishka and Chizhik down for a safe landing. The men gave a great cheer.

The space dog program was back on track, but behind schedule. To make up time, Smelaya's flight was scheduled four days later. There was no training those last few days, just rest and walks twice a day. Smelaya and Ryzhik got a final walk the afternoon before the launch. Only on that occasion, Smelaya did something she had never done before—she ran away. One minute the man with the thick glasses could see her wagging tail poking from a bush, and the next minute she was gone. He searched for her for nearly an hour before going back to report her disappearance.

He was embarrassed, for himself since she had been with him when she disappeared, but for Smelaya, too. They were making history here, advancing science, and everyone had to play their part. It wouldn't do for "Brave One" to run away.

Days were long this time of year, so the search for Smelaya continued well into the evening hours. But as night began to fall, they had still not found her. The other handlers gave up searching. They reminded the man with the thick glasses that the dogs would have to be loaded into the rocket in a few hours. They said that another dog would have to go instead of Smelaya.

For the next few hours the man drove around the plains surrounding the launch facility. He thought he saw Smelaya in a hundred shadows cast by the bright moon. But when he stopped to call her name, he heard only the lonely howl of a wolf far in the distance. That made him shudder. A hungry wolf would make a quick meal of little Smelaya.

In the middle of the night, with launch time rapidly approaching, he drove back to the kennel. Another dog would have to be selected. Since all the flights had been planned and the dogs trained for their chosen flight, it was no easy thing to rearrange them.

"They want to use Nochka as the replacement," one of the other handlers told the man when he returned. The man with the thick glasses nodded; Smelaya was going to miss her chance to fly. The history books would say, "Space Dog Smelaya did not fly on a rocket because she ran away just before it was launched." He headed to the kennel to retrieve the other dog. As he was taking her from the cage, he heard a familiar barking—Smelaya! There she stood at his feet. She had found her own way back home. She looked so innocent, her one droopy ear laying on its side. He quickly put Nochka back in her cage and took Smelaya for her date with history.

Everything was rushed now. The dogs were dressed and hurried to the launch pad. A metal panel sealed them into their capsule. Final preparation of the rocket and testing of the equipment, took two more hours.

One minute until launch. A movie camera on the rocket would record the dogs all through the flight, but scientists would not be able to view the film until it was recovered after the flight. Ten seconds to go. But the man with the thick glasses had seen film from the earlier flights. He knew exactly what Smelaya and Ryzhik were about to experience. Two seconds. One second. A flash of light, then the boom of the engine blasting out its fiery tail.

The man knew that at that very moment a powerful noise and vibration were spreading throughout the frame of the rocket, stronger than anything the dogs had experienced in training. He knew the look of fright that would be in their eyes. He had seen it in training. If they were not strapped securely in place, they would be straining to get away, giving into their fear. A clock in the camera's view would show the passing seconds as the force of acceleration pressed the dogs more and more tightly against the floor of their capsule, until they were paralyzed by the unseen weight.

It took but a minute for the rocket to burn up all of its fuel. At that moment, the dogs' heads would suddenly jump up, as the period of weightlessness began. The rocket was coasting now, its speed carrying it higher for a few more minutes. Now their straps were keeping them from floating around the capsule. They would be sitting quietly.

The rocket climbed higher but was quickly losing speed, until finally it hung motionless for just a moment, before beginning its fall back to earth. As the man with the thick glasses knew, this would be the most difficult part of the flight for Semlaya and Ryzhik. In many ways, getting dogs 63 miles into the atmosphere was a lot easier than returning them safely to earth. Rockets were always being made larger and more powerful, bigger fuel tanks, bigger engines. Soviet scientists would know how to orbit a dog in space long before they knew how to return it. Once you had dogs that high in the atmosphere, how did you get them back safely? Many different experiments were yet to come on astronaut recovery.

The type of capsule carrying Smelaya and Ryzhik did not fall smoothly back down through the atmosphere, but shifted position. Later models would have stabilizing fins, but this one turned sideways, upside down, rotated and rolled. As the capsule turned the dogs this way and that, the force of acceleration once more pushed them around. But it was different than on the rocket ride up. Instead of being pushed in only one direction, now the dogs got pushed in many directions. The dogs might be falling sideways one minute and upside down the next. Film of earlier flights showed some dogs on their backs with paws in the air, then as the capsule changed position in its fall, their back legs lifted higher than their head. Some of the dogs suffered minor cuts and bruises from being bumped about inside their capsule.

When the parachute appeared, the man with the thick glasses gave a great sigh of relief. Old droopy ear had played her part in history. And survived.

Everyone felt better now, after two successful flights. Everything was working as it should as they went into the final two flights. But that good feeling would not last very long. On August 28, tragedy struck again. The rocket carrying Mishka and Chizhik, on their second flight, experienced mechanical problems and crashed, killing both dogs.

Perhaps the man with the thick glasses was more sensitive to the dogs than others, perhaps he was crazy, but he sensed a tension in the kennel. As though word of the deaths had spread among the cages. It <u>was</u> crazy, but...he felt it. Nervous dogs became quiet, quiet dogs could hardly be coaxed from their cages. And then, they had a another runaway. Bobik ran away just as Smelaya had done. Only Bobik didn't return. The night before Bobik was supposed to be launched, when her cage still stood empty, a stray dog from the neighborhood was recruited, given a quick spin in the centrifuge as her only training and suited up for the launch. They called her ZIB, which were the initials for the Russian words for "substitute for missing dog Bobik."

ZIB and a dog named Neputevyy made a successful flight on September 3, 1951, finishing the first series of flights in the dog program. Nine dogs had stepped into the history of space travel by flying on those early rockets. Four of those dogs gave their lives in man's quest for knowledge. Scientists would be able to use what they had learned from these flights to move one step closer to human space travel. But they still had many more things to learn before that could happen.

6

Dogs Go Higher

Smelaya's old crew mate, Ryzhik, shook herself, spraying water around the room. Her fur poked up at odd angles. She and a new dog named Lisa (This was the second dog named Lisa.) had just been bathed and now stood before a heater drying off. A whole crew of workers fluttered around them. The man with the thick glasses rubbed Ryzhik with a towel, while Lisa got a brush down.

It was the summer of 1954, three years since the first dog launches. A new series of rocket flights was underway using a new capsule, a new space suit, and a new way of returning the dogs to earth. Animal astronauts continued to be the pioneers of rocket travel. The United States had achieved its first animal astronaut success in the fall of 1951, recovering a monkey from a suborbital flight. However, the U.S. had not flown another animal since then, and would not again until 1958.

From 1951 until 1958, only the Soviet Union was flying animals astronauts. And, very, very much would happen in those seven years. Fifteen times dogs would fly in rockets in those years, and they would go higher than any living creature had ever gone, right to the very edge of space. History would be made when Sputnik I, a small metal ball full of radio equipment, launched by the Soviet Union, became the first object to circle the earth in space. It was called a "satellite," and perhaps more than anything, it began what would later be called the "Space Race," between the Soviet Union and the United States. One month after Sputnik, came the most historic flight of all—a dog would become the first living creature to conquer space. But all of that was still a few years away. On this day, two dogs were being readied to ride a rocket 63 miles high.

When the dogs were dry, a medical technician smeared grease at spots on their bodies where electrodes were then attached. Bandages held the wires in place while each dog was slipped into a thin, green shirt. Next came a vest that had sensors in it to measure their breathing. A rubber tube stuck out the back, holding all of the wires that would later be connected to instruments in the capsule. These would record pulse rate, breathing, blood pressure, and body temperature. A movie camera would make a record of the dogs' behavior. The dogs calmly accepted all the attention of the fussing humans. Ryzhik had already flown on two flights this summer, one of them with Lisa.

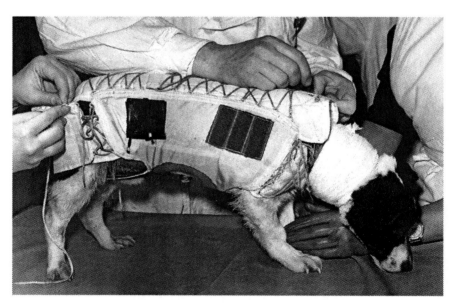

One type of space suit worn by the dogs. This is Veterok, outfitted as he would have been for his record-breaking 22–day flight in 1966.
Novosti (London).

Kozyavka peers through the bubble helmet of her "pressure suit."
For some sub-orbital flights, the capsule was not pressurized, and
dogs were dressed in pressurized suits like this one.
Novosti (London).

"Thirty minutes," said the man with the thick glasses. He carried a
clipboard and checked off each part of the procedure as it was completed. Next on his list, it said, "Sanitation Suit." What looked like a
pair of short stretch pants were pulled over the lower bodies of both
dogs. An attached rubber hose would allow them to urinate during the
flight.

It was the middle of the night, four hours before launch, when the
dogs arrived at the launch pad. They had to dress in one final layer of
clothing—the pressure suits. The pressure suit was a new piece of
equipment for the space dogs. It looked like a bag. It was made of three
layers of rubber fabric, with extensions for the dog's front feet. Ryzhik
and Lisa were slipped inside their suits and fastened there with straps.
Their heads poked through a metal collar. Next, a clear plastic helmet
was fastened over Ryzhik's head then Lisa's and locked in place on the

collar. It looked as though a large bubble had swallowed each of them. The helmet had a small "porthole" that would open automatically to let in air when they descended below 13,000 feet, during the parachute return. On the first series of flights, the dogs had flown in a sealed capsule that contained its own air supply. On these flights, the dogs would carry their air supply in the pressurized suits. The suits could also adjust the temperature hotter or colder to keep the dogs comfortable.

Looking very much like alien space creatures, the dogs were fastened into the cramped capsule on the top of the rocket. Men connected wires from the dogs to the equipment in the capsule, then everything was tested and retested. Radio signals on the dogs' health would be transmitted to the ground during the flight.

By the time the dogs were completely settled in the rocket and the workers withdrew, the first hint of morning glowed on the horizon. Time for blast off. Lost in the roar and fiery light of this more powerful R-1D rocket, Ryzhik and Lisa climbed swiftly to the top of their ride at 63 miles high.

This series of rocket launches was testing new ways of returning the astronauts. There had always been a question about whether it was better to eject the dogs from the capsule high in the atmosphere or let them fall to a lower altitude and eject them there. On this flight, they tried both ways. As the rocket started its fall back to earth, a small explosion shot Lisa from the rocket aboard a metal tray. A huge parachute opened. For over an hour she floated slowly to earth, carried by the wind, and landed nearly 50 miles away from the launch site.

Meanwhile, Ryzhik stayed in the rocket as it fell toward the ground, picking up speed as it went. About 25 miles above the surface of the earth, Ryzhik, too was ejected from the rocket. Her ejection capsule was supposed to fall until it was about 2 ½ miles above the ground, when its parachute would open.

But tragedy struck again on this day. Only one parachute blossomed in the sky and floated safely home. While one silvery piece of metal, with space dog Ryzhik attached, crashed into the ground and took her life.

When the man with the thick glasses went home from work that night he was greeted at the door by his pet dog, barking and jumping up his leg. He ruffled the fur on her neck and smoothed her droopy ear. "Well, girl," he said, "your old friend Ryzhik is gone. One of those accidents." The tone of his voice momentarily calmed Smelaya. Then she snuggled under his hand for more petting. Yes, space dog Smelaya had become a household pet. She was considered too high strung and nervous for the longer flights that were to come. Her days in the space program were over. The man had adopted her, pleased to have a space dog in his home. A number of the space dogs would eventually be adopted by those who worked in the program.

The man had always looked at the space dog program as a great honor for the dogs, just as he considered it a great honor for himself. He had no patience for the animal protectors who said that dogs should not be used in scientific experiments. After all, this was the new frontier of knowledge, and they were pioneers blazing a trail into space. Men would soon be going through the very same training. They would he shaken and spun around; they would breath pressurized air, experience weightlessness, and sit in cramped capsules for days—just like the dogs.

Odd, the man thought, as he stroked Smelaya's head. He used to think that all of this training was only for the dogs, when in reality it was for the humans, too. The scientists, veterinarians, engineers, *everyone* working in the space program was in training. If the dogs had to learn how to handle acceleration, vibration, and weightlessness, then the humans had to learn how to make rockets fly higher and bring astronauts back alive.

Apparently, the dogs were learning faster than the human. All of the medical evidence gathered from the dogs so far, showed that they experienced no physical problems during the flights. That information allowed more serious thought to be given to humans following in their footsteps. It was about this time that planning began for human flights, with much attention being given to the best way to return the astronauts safely. Should their capsule separate from the rocket at low altitudes or high? Should rockets be used to slow its descent? A helicopter-like rotor blade was even under consideration. The current flights would continue to test capsule separation at different altitudes.

A rocket sled was used to train the dogs for this experience. It tested the physical effects of extreme acceleration and deceleration. Let's look in on veteran space dog, Albina on a rocket sled ride. Fluffy white Albina is suited up in all of her flight clothes, bubble helmet on her head, then strapped onto the sled. There is a loud crack and a mighty whoosh as a rocket shoots the sled along rails for a short ride at incredible speed. Then just as quickly, it is brought to a stop. Veterinarians rush to lift her out. Albina wears a dazed look and can not stand on her own. The vets examine her skin, eyes, and ears to look for bleeding that is sometimes caused by this test. There is some, but nothing serious. X-rays are taken to check for broken bones, but none are found. Minutes later, she appears to have recovered. Then its back to the kennel for some rest. One more day in the life of a space dog.

◆   ◆   ◆

When flights resumed the following year, it would be on another new rocket, the R-1Ye rocket. The R-1Ye rocket flew six times, between January 1955 and June 1956. Some of the original space dogs had been waiting a long time for their chance to fly. Now it was here. Albina flew three times during this series of launches, Kozyavka flew twice. When these two dogs flew together, on the last flight in this series, it marked the end of era. A great deal had been learned in the first five years of the dog flights. Now it was time to move to the next level, to go closer to space. Albina and Kozyavka had been trained with the "even tempered" dogs, those picked for longer flights, but now there would be only two categories of dogs in training—rocket dogs and satellite dogs. Rocket dogs would take higher flights into the atmosphere, and satellite dogs would actually go into space.

An even more powerful rocket had been developed for these flights, the R-2A. This would carry the dogs twice as high as they had ever gone, up to 125 miles, to the very edge of space, to a region of the earth's atmosphere called the "thermosphere." This was such a forbidding place that it posed a new problem for the scientists. In the lower thermosphere, starting at an altitude of 74 miles, the temperature can be a frigid -93 degrees. Higher in the thermosphere, where it is affected by energy from the sun, temperatures can climb to a sizzling 3,000 degrees. How did you protect an astronaut from temperatures that could jump from extreme cold to extreme heat in minutes?

With this rocket, the recovery system would separate the dog capsule from the rocket at the very peak of its flight. The capsule would then free fall from there—over 120 miles—to within a few miles of earth, where three parachutes would open to lower it the rest of the way.

The man with the thick glasses entered the kennel. He was now in charge of dog training. He made up their training schedules, placed dogs into groups depending on their personality, and decided which dogs went on which flights. The kennel had grown quite a bit over the past few years, with the addition of many new recruits. He read the names on the cages: Dzhoyna, Knopka, Rita. These were some of the rocket dogs. And over here: Malek, Lisichka, Strelka, Palma, some of the satellite dogs.

The satellite dogs received all the training of the rocket dogs plus additional training. Their flights would last for days, possibly weeks. So, they had to be especially calm. In training, the rocket dogs would remain in a confinement capsule for several hours, while the satellite dogs would stay there for 10 to 15 days.

For the first time on these longer flights, the dogs would be fed during the flight. Part of training therefore involved learning how to eat from a mechanical feeding machine called an automat. The automat was built into the floor of the capsule right in front of the dog. At a set time, a conveyor belt moved a container of food into position, a door snapped open, and the dog could eat the special dog food designed for space travel. If they were fed regular dog food, in the zero gravity of space, the food would float up and out of the food dish. The dog would have to try to snap it from the air. The problem was the same with water. If a dog tried to lick water out of a bowl in space, it would separate into droplets and float around the capsule.

Kozyavka, Linda, and Malyshka, who had recently completed sub-orbital flights, photographed during a press conference in 1957.
Novosti (London).

Scientists solved this problem by preparing a special diet of meat, fat and grain mixed with a lot of water. The food looked like jelly and stuck to the sides of the feeding box. In eating this mixture, the dogs got both food and water. But the dogs had to be taught to eat this strange food and to eat it from this strange and noisy device. The automat made a loud whirring noise as the food moved into position, then the lid opened with a loud click. Eventually, when they were hungry enough, they learned to eat from the automatic feeder.

The flights that went to an altitude of 125 miles began in May 1957 and were marred by only one tragedy. The dogs Ryzhaya and Dzhoyna lost their lives on the second flight, on May 24. This series of launches finished on August 25, when Belka and Modnitsa made a successful flight.

The space dog program was about to be overshadowed by a rocket launch happening at a different launch site, in a part of the Soviet Union called Kazakhstan. On October 4, 1957 the Soviet Union launched a metal ball the size of a grapefruit into orbit around the earth. Named Sputnik, this satellite was the first object ever to be shot into space. Mankind's longtime dream, to travel in space, had just taken one giant step closer to becoming reality.

Everything changed after Sputnik. Newspapers around the world celebrated the event, bringing much publicity to the Soviet space program. It seemed as though the future had suddenly arrived. A man-made object had flown in space. But before the world could fully absorb the accomplishment of Sputnik, the leader of the Soviet Union, Nikita Khrushchev, had another surprise.

The surprise began to unfold in a Moscow radio station in October 1957, about two weeks after the launch of Sputnik. Khrushchev stood at one microphone, holding a sheet of paper. He was a large man, in a round sort of way, with a stern face. On this day he beamed with excitement. At the other microphone, stood the man with the thick glasses and one of the space dogs.

At a signal from the radio engineer, Khrushchev made his stunning announcement. First he boasted about his country's great accomplishment in launching the world's first earth-orbiting satellite, Sputnik, earlier that month. But now the Soviet Union had even more ambitious plans, he explained. He paused to glance over at the man with the thick glasses, who drew the dog a step closer to the microphone. The man was extremely nervous; the dog gave the microphone a casual sniff.

"In two weeks," Khrushchev continued, "to mark the 40th anniversary of the Soviet Union, our scientists will launch a second satellite into orbit, only this one will contain a living organism—a dog. That dog is here right now." Khrushchev motioned and the man with the thick glasses held up a piece of food, which always made the dog bark. "Her name is Kudryavka," Krushchev explained, "the world's first space traveler."

A half hour later, the man with the thick glasses was driving home, Kudryavka in the car seat beside him. That broadcast had been such a silly event, and yet…he held his hand above Kudryavka's head, making her bark…and yet, Kudryavka had just announced the space dog program to the world. For six years the space dogs had flown in almost complete secrecy. Now, the eyes of the world would focus on their accomplishments.

7

Laika, Space Heroine

A young woman entered the office of the man with the thick glasses and handed him a telegram. He had never received a telegram before. He tore it open and read its simple message, "We are waiting." That was all it said. He took a deep breath because he knew exactly what it meant.

The message was typical of the Soviet space program, where everything was TOP SECRET. No mention was ever made of rockets, launch sites, or space dogs in telegrams or over the phone. Even in conversation with each other, scientists were careful. It was thought that spies might be anywhere and could learn secret information.

The man with the thick glasses telephoned his assistant. "It's time. Get the dogs ready to leave immediately."

Since the launch the previous month of Sputnik, everything had happened so quickly. Newspapers around the world had praised the achievement. In fact it was that publicity that had prompted the Soviet leader, Nikita Khrushchev, to announce that the Soviet Union would next launch a living being into space, and it would happen in only one month.

Prepare for an orbital flight in one month?! An orbital flight with a live passenger?! Something that had never been done before?! The scientists were in a panic at such an incredible challenge. In fact, the scientists who had just worked long and hard to launch Sputnik, had been given a much-deserved vacation. They had to be called quickly back to the secret launch site in central Russia called Baikonur, from where Sputnik had been launched, to work around the clock to prepare a satellite that would carry a dog into orbit.

The telegram the man held in his hands meant that the launch was about to unfold. They were ready for the space dog who would fly in that historic rocket. Several dogs had been in rigorous training for many month as "satellite dogs," to undertake a mission just like this. But which one would make this flight? After the most rigorous testing, the honor had gone to a dog who had never flown before. Her name had originally been Kudryavka (Little Curly), but during the last few weeks, the workers had renamed her Laika, which meant "barker." She was a short-haired white dog with black spots and slightly droopy ears. Like many of the other dogs, she had been a stray, picked up off the streets of Moscow. She had earned a reputation as the most even-tempered of all of the space dogs. She would patiently endure all of the training without complaint. Confined in her tiny capsule, circling the earth for many days, would require a great deal of patience indeed.

By that afternoon, the man was on an airplane on his way to the launch site. Two dogs traveled with him. Although only Laika had been selected to make this flight, veteran space dog Albina would be her backup. If for some reason Laika would be unable to make the flight, Albina would take her place.

The man passed the time during his flight by reading the newspaper. There were still many articles about Sputnik in newspapers and magazines. The American President Eisenhower, said that his country would shortly launch its own satellite. The term "space race" would later be used to describe the competition between the United States and the Soviet Union to be the first with each new step that led closer to placing a human in space. The launch of Sputnik had really been the opening gun at the start of the space race.

Soldiers met the man's plane and drove him to the launch site. They pinned a badge onto his coat with the number 72 on it. "You are 72," the soldier said. "No names here, only numbers."

The Soviet space program had always been cloaked in secrecy. The Soviets did not want foreign governments to know the location of launch sites or learn information about rockets. These same facilities and rockets could also be used for military purposes in the event of war, and military secrets were the most carefully guarded of all. Telephone lines could be tapped, high altitude foreign airplanes could fly overhead snapping pictures, spies could be among the workers. Even loyal scientists who knew too much might carelessly let slip important information in a conversation. So no one at Baikonur would know the name of the man in the thick glasses who took care of the dog. To them he would simply be 72.

The next day, October 31, 1957, Laika took her morning walk in the brisk fall air, along with Albina. The man gave them extra time to play. He threw sticks for them to chase and roughed up their fur. Laika rolled onto her back to get her stomach scratched.

When they returned, Laika's long preparation began. Her fur was washed with an alcohol solution and combed. Then on went her vest, sanitation suit, and the harness that would hold her in place. The workers had done this many times before, but they seemed more quiet and serious on this occasion.

Laika let out a few barks as number 72 checked her over. She seemed more ready for play than for the serious business of space travel. They took the short ride from the kennel to the launch pad. Carrying Laika in a traveling cage, the man stood on the ground at the foot of the mighty rocket that would carry her into space and stared up at the nose cone. Laika would travel aboard the SS-6 rocket. Wide as a house at the ground, it tapered to a gleaming white nose cone 110 feet high. A massive machine, it represented the best in rocket technology. It was large enough, the man realized, to carry a human astronaut into space. And that was exactly what the dog flights were designed to do, pave the way for manned flights.

Scaffolding surrounded the giant rocket so that workers could be close to whatever part of the rocket they had to work on. Number 72 climbed to the highest level to inspect the dog capsule. It was a large metal cylinder. The first satellite, Sputnik, had been the size of a grapefruit and weighed a few pounds. This capsule weighed 1,100 pounds! It didn't take much imagination to realize that humans, too, would soon travel in space. The same equipment, the same principles that allowed a dog to travel in space would let humans do it too.

The capsule had been fitted with all the equipment needed to keep a living, breathing creature alive in the dark and frigid realm of space. The interior of the capsule looked like a nest of high cushions, covered in soft cloth. A metal plate in the cork floor indicated where Laika's meals would be delivered from the automatic feeder. Heaters under the floor would keep her warm, and another device would generate the oxygen she needed to breath. A TV camera pointed right at her head would broadcast images of her back to the ground.

Laika was placed into her capsule around noon, straps fastened, wires and sanitation tubes connected. Everything got checked and rechecked. There was no room for error. For each item completed, the man put a checkmark on the list he carried on his clipboard. Throughout all of this, Laika remained her usual calm self, as though this was only another day of training. She had just enough room to lay down, sit, or stand. As the metal hood of the capsule was lowered into place, Laika strained at her harness and barked in protest.

The assembled capsule looked like a large barrel, with a small glass porthole in the end, which allowed a glimpse of Laika inside. Now she only had to wait inside her capsule for the launch, which was three days away.

Monitoring equipment stood on the scaffolding outside the capsule. Lights and dials blinked and fluttered, indicating proper air circulation and temperature, and recording her physical responses. During the flight this information would be radioed to earth, but for now it allowed workers to watch Laika's condition while she waited for launch.

Laika being fitted into her air-tight capsule just before being
launched into space, November 1957. *Novosti (London)*.

The next day, the man with the thick glasses climbed the scaffolding
again to check on Laika. The medical monitoring equipment left a
record on long spools of paper. There he could see that her breathing
had been normal. Her heart beat had ranged from 68 to 120, within
the normal range. Peering through the thick glass of the port hole, he
could barely see Laika sitting in the dark capsule. With an outside
switch, he activated the feeding device. Laika jerked up immediately at
the noise, which meant that she still had her appetite. When the door
snapped open, she gobbled down the food.

All of the wires, machines, glowing lights, and strips of paper gave
the oddest impression—that Laika was actually a part of this great
machine, rather than just a passenger. The man with the thick glasses
was only a number, 72, just another piece of equipment. But Laika was

the warm and furry heart powering the mightiest rocket in the world. When the man backed away, he felt his own heart racing.

On the evening of November 2, the man climbed the scaffold for one last look at Laika. She would blast into space at 5:30 the next morning. According to the medical equipment, she was still in good condition. Through the porthole, he saw her laying there, maybe sleeping. It must be getting cramped for her, he thought. How much she would like a good run in a field. He rubbed at the glass of the porthole with the sleeve of his coat to clear some dust, and the motion caught Laika's attention. The feeble light blinked off her eyes. She stood up immediately and strained at her straps, barking in excited recognition.

This is the point where he would usually rough the fur on her neck. She loved that and would push against his leg to make him continue. He could see that she expected that, and he felt bad that he couldn't give her that little bit of play. He felt worse at that moment because he knew the secret of this flight. He knew exactly what this space craft was capable of doing and what it was not. But no one spoke about that. He raised his hand to say goodbye. At this moment she was just another dog, a mutt grabbed from the streets of Moscow. Tomorrow she would be the most famous dog in the history of the world.

She began her trip into history at sunrise, November 3, 1957. The man with the thick glasses sat behind a desk full of machines that received information about Laika radioed back from the capsule. Seconds after launch, her heart rate jumped to 260 beats per minute and her breathing to 4 times its normal rate. That was high, but still within the safe range. Fortunately, her actual flight into space was a short one. Within minutes of launch, the engines used up all of their fuel. One second the rocket would be blasting Laika with a deafening roar and shaking her almost beyond endurance, and then it would all stop. Silence would surround her as the rocket sped smoothly towards space and slipped into orbit at more than 900 miles above the earth. At that altitude, her space craft would travel at 18,000 miles an hour and orbit the earth every 102 minutes. If everything worked properly.

Back in the launch building, scientists crowded around a small television screen, watching scratchy, grey lines. Had she gotten into orbit? Was she ok? Someone adjusted a knob, and the dark form of Laika's head came into focus on the screen. The quality of the picture from the onboard TV camera was bad, but they could see her head moving. She even barked. "Yea," they cheered. She was alive. She had survived being launched into earth orbit. They had done it. They had proved that they could create a capsule that provided all of the life support necessary for space travel. They wore broad smiles and slapped each other on the back.

The man with the thick glasses studied the TV image. Just as he liked to study the dogs in their kennel, so too he hope to read in the TV picture clues to her well being. Laika was completely weightless now and would remain so for as long as she stayed in orbit. The awkward movements of her head and legs showed her struggle to adjust to zero gravity. But, she had survived. A living creature was actually flying in space. It took his breath away, and he found himself unable to move for an instant.

During each 90 minute orbit, the capsule flew above the Soviet Union for almost 30 minutes. All along its route, ground stations picked up its radio signals and forwarded them to the waiting scientists at Baikonur. On the second orbit, the TV camera showed Laika moving around a lot more. Her breathing and heart rate had jumped and she was clearly uncomfortable. "The capsule is overheating," one scientist said, and the man with the thick glasses hurried over to check the readings—90 degrees and rising. Laika could not hold out long in such heat. The heater in the capsule could have warmed her if she was cold, but there was no way to cool her.

During the next orbit, the situation had gotten worse. The medical instruments clearly showed her distress. She no longer squirmed about. Her body temperature was too high, her breathing shallow. Entirely on her own in the vastness of space, nothing could be done for her.

This grainy TV image of Laika was broadcast back to earth during her flight. She appears alert here, but a few hours after she went into orbit, overheating of the capsule would take her life.
Novosti (London).

The man with the thick glasses anxiously awaited the return of the satellite during the next orbit. Finally, when the fourth orbit again brought Sputnik 2 into Soviet air space, and the tracking stations began to monitor the satellite's radio signals, they showed no life signs. Breathing and heart rate had stopped. The man studied the monitors for the longest time, hoping some weak signal would appear. But nothing came in. Only hours into the flight, space had claimed its first victim.

The following morning the official announcement went out from Moscow. The Soviet Union had launched its second space craft, Sputnik 2, the message said, and this one included a live passenger, a dog named Laika. It was a great advancement in man's effort to explore space. Laika's death was not mentioned.

Newspapers around the world splashed it on their front pages. The official start of mankind's long-held dream of traveling to the stars, they said. Sputnik 2 was much larger than Sputnik 1 and easier to see from the ground, the newspapers explained. They gave their readers the exact time when it would pass over their location. Scientists and broadcasting companies around the world tracked the telltale "beep, beep, beep" radio signal of the satellite over the following days, just as they had done with Sputnik 1. The thought of Laika making her lonely orbits of earth stirred people's imagination. Millions of people around the world woke in the middle of the night so they could look for the satellite that carried the space dog, the most famous dog in history.

◆　　　◆　　　◆

The alarm clock jangled in the bedroom of the man with the thick glasses. He threw on the clothes that he had laid out the night before. He donned a heavy coat, hat, and gloves, then went outside. Not a single cloud obscured the night sky. The constellation Orion glittered brightly overhead, as did the smudge of light that was the Milky Way.

Though Laika had died, her capsule still sailed among the stars. If you were waiting at just the right time, and the weather cooperated, you could see it pass over. He checked his watch, then scanned the horizon. At precisely the predicted time, there it was—a bright dot inching its way across the blackness of space. Almost as bright as the brightest star, the satellite worked like an artificial moon, reflecting sunlight back to earth. Seeing it like this, sailing across the sky, drove home the significance of the event. At this very moment, thousand of eyes—tens of thousands of eyes—in the Soviet Union would be watching this very same spectacle. And as the satellite continued in its orbit, people would crawl from their beds in darkness in other countries, to step into their back yards and turn their eyes towards the heavens to see Laika sail overhead, not knowing that she had already given her life.

In his imagination, the man could clearly picture the last time he had seen Laika, when she had gotten so excited to glimpse him through the port hole of her space capsule. He had known the sad truth even then—that she would not survive this flight. Scientists had achieved the great technological success of placing a living creature into orbit, but they had not yet developed a way to return capsules from orbit. Laika had been given enough air and food to keep her alive for about a week. Then she would have died up there alone in space. The problem with overheating had simply taken her life more quickly.

For another five months, Laika's capsule continued to orbit the earth, and occasionally the man with the thick glasses would still wake in the middle of the night to watch it pass overhead. On April 13, 1958, after completing 2,370 orbits, some 62 million miles, the capsule burned up on reentry into the earth's atmosphere.

8

Satellite Dogs

"They will be here in 30 minutes," the assistant told the man with the thick glasses as they hurried into yet another room of the launch bunker. Men stood around electronic equipment, studying gauges and reading the jittery lines painting themselves across tiny TV screens.

"Yes, yes. You reminded me of that 30 seconds ago." Someone handed the man a clipboard for his signature, another directed his attention to equipment that monitored the electrical circuits of the big rocket sitting on the launch pad.

"It's just that we should be getting to the reception area."

"Work on a launch doesn't stop because we are getting visitors."

"Yes, but..." The man held up his hand to stop the assistant from completing his thought. "Five more minutes, then we will go to greet our guests."

The man with the thick glasses took a deep breath to calm himself, then plunged back into the work. Although the launch was not until the next morning, the space dogs Chaika and Lisichka were already in their capsule atop the rocket. It was a hot day in July 1960. Nine successful suborbital flights over a three year period had led up to this moment—the first orbital flight since Laika had flown in 1957, almost three years ago.

The space dog program had grown considerably over those years. In the control room engineers nervous about the rocket huddled around electronic equipment. A meteorologist drew symbols on a wall map that showed weather patterns. Someone gave orders over the phone about loading fuel into the rocket. But, the man in the thick glasses only had to worry about the dogs. His dogs were going back into orbit, and every detail of their health and safety had to be perfect.

This was the era of the "satellite dogs," those even-tempered dogs who had trained the longest and hardest, because their flights would be longer and more demanding than those early dog flights. The satellite dogs had begun flying in August of 1958, with a suborbital flight by the dogs Kusachka and Palma. The larger R5-A rocket lifted some of these flights to an altitude of 280 miles to test the new recovery system that again ejected the capsule for a parachute descent to earth. It was the same recovery system that would be used on the first manned flight. Five flights in 1958, two in 1959, including one on which a rabbit named Marfusha rode along with the dogs Otvazhnaya and Snezhinka, plus two flights earlier this year.

As fast as they sent up flights, there was always pressure from above to do it faster. The United States had launched its first satellite in January 1958. It was sending monkeys on sub-orbital flights. In April 1959 it had selected its first group of space pilots, the seven Mercury astronauts. That same year, in much more secrecy, the Soviet Union began to train its own small group of pilots, or "cosmonauts," to fly in space. Testing also began on a space capsule named Vostok that would carry the first human into space. The space race had shifted into high gear.

Now, in the summer of 1960, the Soviet Union was about to once again orbit dogs in space, take them back to where Laika had been in 1957. Only this time they would bring them back alive. Chaika and Lisichka would be the first living beings to fly in space and return to earth. The successful completion of this mission was one of the few hurdles remaining before a man flew in space.

From the other side of the room, the assistant waved his hands frantically and pointed to his watch. This time the man nodded his head.

Outside, a photographer had lined up the space dogs. "Bring them in closer," he said, pointing to a spot in front of his camera. Two of the dogs, Belyanka and Malek trotted over to where he had pointed, but the others needed to be shooed along by the handlers. They had just managed to all settle down—Kusachka, Belka, Otvazhnaya, Palma, Pestraya, Zemchuznaya, and Strelka—when a bus pulled into view down the road. It drove directly towards them, its brakes squeaking it to a stop, its door popping open. Out stepped five men. These were the men who had been chosen by the Soviet Union to fly in space, the cosmonauts, and they were here to watch their first rocket launch.

The onboard movie camera watches the "satellite dogs" Belyanka
and Pestraya during their suborbital flight in August 1958.
Novosti (London).

The line of five cosmonauts stood face to face across from the line of space dogs, as though they both expected something important to happen. Finally, one of the cosmonauts stooped and extended his hand. None of the dogs moved. "Come here little one," he said to Pestraya. She shot him a curious glance, but did not move. He beckoned to another one, but she too was not tempted.

The cosmonauts looked at each other in a way that suggested that these were pretty strange dogs. A few of the others attempted the same thing with the same result. The man with the thick glasses was pleasantly surprised. His dogs were behaving like perfect little soldiers, well disciplined. Next to the humans, who were now joking and laughing at their inability to make the dogs respond, the dogs seemed more serious, more professional. They were the experienced rocket fliers. Who were these noisy humans, but a bunch of rookies in training?

The cosmonauts lined up behind the space dogs for the photographer. The event didn't seem serious to them. They joked with each other and tried to play with the dogs. But when the photographers said "Ready," everyone froze for a moment, and the flash caught them.

Few scenes could have better captured the current moment in space history. The present belonged to the space dogs. They had been flying rockets for years, had orbited the earth in space; two more of them sat in a rocket on the launch pad about to go back into space and to make a final test of the capsule and equipment that would soon carry humans.

However, the future belonged to these cosmonauts. All of them were seasoned pilots, but they would still have to undergo months of intense training to prepare them for what they would experience on a rocket ride into space. In fact, it was training very similar to what the space dogs had already endured. Many of the lessons learned in the preparation of dogs to fly in space could be used to better train humans to do the same thing.

The cosmonauts spent the rest of the day touring the dog training facility and watching the preparations for the launch. From their own training, they were familiar with such equipment as the centrifuge and cramped capsules, but they were very curious about the rocket sled and vibratable.

But their main interest on this occasion was the launch. They wanted to see what actually happened on a launch. What was the rocket like? How did the ground crew prepare it? How were the dogs positioned in the capsule? What procedures were followed in the count down to launch? Some of them had never even seen a rocket before. This was a valuable part of their training. They spent time at the launch pad and in the bunker, and had many questions for the workers and scientists.

The presence of the cosmonauts brought a new level of excitement and purpose to the workers, reminding them that soon men would travel aboard these rockets. All of them felt proud to be working on such an important program, proud too that Soviet rocket science was leading the way for the rest of the world.

As with other launches, this one was scheduled at dawn. It was past midnight when the man in the thick glasses glanced at his watch. The cosmonauts seemed too excited to worry about sleep. His own body tingled with nervous energy. Although he needed some rest, he knew he wouldn't be able to sleep. He stepped outside to breath in the warm, night air.

Stars glittered in a black velvet sky—perfect launch weather. In the distance, flood lights lit the rocket on the launch pad. Distant voices of men at work and the low rumble of truck engines drifted to his ears from the area of the rocket. And another sound, too. Barking.

For a moment, the wind played a trick on him, making it seem as though the barking came from the direction of the rocket. As though Lisichka or Chaika had second thoughts about taking this rocket ride. But, no, the sound came from the kennel. He headed in that direction.

A wire fence surrounded a group of wooden cages. The dog's name appeared on the door of each cage. One of the handlers had taken to painting a little rocket on the door for each flight a dog had taken. Here was Otvazhnaya, fast asleep, who had three rockets painted on her door. Last month she had flown with Malek and a rabbit named Marfusha. He walked down the row of cages, seeing that they all were asleep.

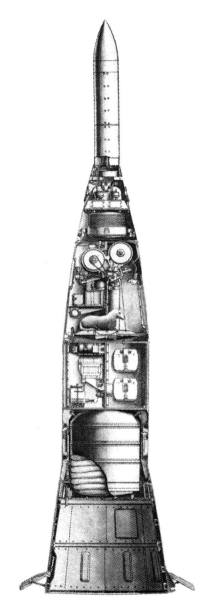

This cut-away drawing of the R-2A rocket shows the position of the
dog capsule. The movie camera, directly above the dog's head,
recorded the dog's behavior for later study. *RKK Energia.*

He thought it was important to visit the dogs and came here often. Back in his office he had mountains of information about them. He knew how many hours they had spent in isolation capsules and how many times they had spun in the centrifuge. He knew exactly how fast their heart beat and how many breaths they took when the force of an accelerating rocket squashed them onto the floor like a load of bricks. He had watched hours of movies of their behavior during the flights, when noise blasted their ears and vibration shook them and weightlessness made them float light as a feather.

But these were only numbers and pictures. He also liked to follow them back to their cages and watch carefully how they behaved. See the real flesh and blood dogs. Were they tired or playful? Confused or nervous? Were they withdrawn? Were they hungry? Sometimes he felt that he could learn more this way than from all the charts and numbers back in his office, as though the behavior of the dogs told him important things if he just looked carefully enough.

On this night, all of the dogs slept peacefully, except one. When he came to the cage of Strelka, she whimpered and pushed her nose through the wire on her door. "What's bothering you, Strelka?" He removed her from the cage, looked her over, and petted her. She was fine. He carried her to the fence and held her up for a view of the rocket. "That's what all the commotion is about. There's a launch this morning. You should be used to this by now."

But she would not be comforted by words. When you watched the dogs undergo their training, you came to know their personalities. Strelka and her training companion Belka, had long been identified as some of the easy-going dogs who would do well on long, orbital flights. Although Belka, at 2 ½ years of age, was a year older than Strelka, she behaved more like a puppy, playful and energetic, while Strelka was more calm. And yet the man could think of a dozen times when they changed roles, when Belka would be the quiet one. For example, the first time they were fitted into rubberized space suits and strapped into a capsule, Belka whimpered for a while, then settled right down. But,

Strelka went crazy. She did not like the tight suit and the cramped space. She showed her displeasure by barking and repeatedly trying to bite through the restraining straps to free herself.

That's what you learned by watching the dogs, their personalities, how they would react in different circumstances. What they would endure and when they might break under pressure. You learned, too, which dogs should be paired with which dogs. You saw how one hated vibration while the other tolerated it, how g-forces terrified the second, while another took them without complaint. You could match them up so that one would be strong when the other was not.

The man put Strelka on the ground then sat down himself and let her climb into his lap. He would let her settle down, maybe even fall asleep, then he'd slip her back in the cage. "No use both of us going without sleep," he said. But as she cradled on his legs and began to relax, he made the mistake of closing his eyes and immediately fell asleep.

He dreamt that a dog was licking his face, then he opened his eyes to find that a dog was licking his face. For a moment he didn't realize where he was or what was happening. Then he recognized Strelka and the kennel, and…Oh no! He had fallen asleep. He checked his watch. Fifteen minutes to launch!

He didn't even stop to put Strelka back in her cage, but jumped to his feet and ran to the launch bunker. "We looked all over for you," his assistant said the minute he entered. The workers and the cosmonauts turned his way. He must have looked a sight, having slept on the ground and not shaved or washed up.

Only minutes to go before launch, he took his position beside the machines that monitored the health of the dogs. Everything looked normal. That would change dramatically when the massive rocket engines ignited. The dogs' breathing and heart beats would shoot up under the stress of launch. But he had seen that many times before; it had been well studied. The prize from this flight would be the hours that the dogs spent in the weightlessness of space. Suborbital flights provided only minutes to study the effects of weightlessness. But now they would get to study it carefully.

When the launch count got down to the final seconds, the cosmonauts crowded around the television sets that showed closeups of the rocket on the launch pad. First, the great splash of flames erupted from beneath the rocket. Then it lifted slowly off the pad. The workers had seen it all before and went about their business, but the spectacle hypnotized the cosmonauts. They whispered to each other and pointed to the TV, eyes gleaming with excitement.

Exactly 28 seconds into the flight, a brilliant flash filled the screen. For a few moments everyone froze with disbelief, then the concussion from the blast shook the building and snapped people into frantic activity. Engineers busied themselves over their machines. An eruption of conversation filled the air, people asking questions and shouting orders. What had gone wrong?

The rocket had exploded. The man with the thick glasses hurried outside for a better look, followed by the cosmonauts. Flaming wreckage drifted from the sky. Emergency trucks, sirens screaming, raced to the scene to deal with the fire on the ground and to retrieve the debris. Engineers would study the wreckage to try to understand what had happened.

When all of he pieces had thudded to the ground, all of the cosmonauts looked at him, as though they expected answers. We are inventing space travel as we go along, he wanted to tell them. We don't even know all of the questions, let alone the answers. But he held his tongue. They had enough to deal with without getting the truth.

The man with the thick glasses had his own questions. He went back to his office, where the folders for Chaika and Lisichka sat on his desk. How many dogs had lost their lives? He thought back. A dozen or so over the past nine years. Not many considering the dangerous work. So much had been learned from their sacrifice. And yet…sometimes they put the dogs at needless risk. Rush, always a rush to do things, even before all the equipment was properly tested. But he knew the reason for that. He only had to glance at the clipping tacked to the wall above his desk. "Mercury Seven Astronauts Announced." Someone had sent him the article from an American newspaper when the United States chose the men who would train to go into space. America was racing to get there. Always that had to be in the back of their minds. Beat the Americans.

You are the dog person, he always reminded himself. Make sure they are ready and let others worry about the equipment and politics. He put the folders for Chaika and Lisichka into the "Inactive" file in his storage cabinet. Then he opened the next drawer, where he kept the files of the dogs in training, and drew out two others—Belka and Strelka—and put them on his desk.

In only three weeks, on August 19, 1960, when the problem with the rocket had been fixed, the next orbital flight was ready. Belka and Strelka behaved so pitifully while being loaded into their capsule, whimpering and licking the hands of the workers. Based upon their training, they knew what was coming—noise, isolation, vibration, g-forces—unpleasant things even when you were used to them. What they didn't know, of course, was that they were about to experience all of those unpleasant things at the same time.

The man with the thick glasses held his breath as the rocket lifted off, but the launch went perfectly. A string of radio tracking stations dotted the vast length of the Soviet Union. Each in turn recorded the radio and TV transmissions from the capsule as it flew overhead, until the satellite moved on to the next station. Those reports came back to the launch site headquarters. The rocket placed Belka and Strelka into a 185 mile-high orbit. At that distance and at their speed, they made a complete circle of the earth every 90 minutes. And all the while they were weightless, which offered the perfect opportunity to learn what effects that condition would have on a living being.

"What's wrong with those cameras?" The man with the thick glasses tapped the TV screen, as if that would somehow make the image move. The capsule had just completed its first orbit and was once again passing over the launch site. But, something was wrong. Belka and Strelka floated inches above the floor of the capsule, restrained only by their harnesses. They looked like helium balloons, hovering in air. Hovering in air was to be expected, but they weren't moving. Not turning their heads, not wagging their tails, nothing. They looked stiff as statues. He remembered Laika's quick death and he had to fight back a flash of panic.

A dozen terrible explanations passed through the man's head, but none of them made sense. All of the medical information being radioed back showed that the dogs were doing ok. So, maybe the onboard camera had frozen up, and it kept showing the same picture. But, that wasn't it either, because the camera also showed the capsule clock, ticking off the seconds.

As the satellite continued in its orbit, its transmissions were picked up first by one then another Soviet ground tracking station. "No change. The dogs look paralyzed," they reported. Nor had things changed when a third orbit once more brought the capsule above the launch center. "Heart rate, respiration, blood pressure, everything normal," someone reported. It must be weightlessness, the man with the thick glasses concluded. Apparently, the sensation was so strange and unsettling for the dogs that their bodies just shut down. This could be very bad news for manned space flights if humans reacted the same way?

Finally, on the fourth orbit, Belka gave a little shutter and vomited. It seemed to snap both dogs out of a trance, breaking the spell of the strange experience of being without gravity. For the rest of the flight they looked more alert.

After 18 orbits, the radio command was given for descent. This was an especially critical point in the flight. Bringing dogs safely back from outer space was much more challenging than getting them up there in the first place. The rockets that slow the satellite to drop it out of orbit had to fire at precisely the right moment, for precisely the right length of time. Otherwise the capsule might be traveling too fast and burn up like a meteorite when it hit the atmosphere. Mistakes on timing could also cause the descending capsule to over shoot the recovery area by hundreds or even thousands of miles.

In the launch bunker, radio messages came in from tracking stations and planes and cars in the recovery area—everyone was ready. Rockets fired again to further slow the capsule and begin its final descent. At 4.3 miles above the ground, the container carrying Belka and Strelka separated from the capsule and parachutes opened to lower it to earth.

Far down range, some farmers working in a field saw a mysterious object float out of the sky? When they ran over to where it had landed, they found what looked like a bomb, a metal casing five feet long and two feet wide. Russian writing on the outside requested that the location of the object be reported immediately to a certain address in Moscow.

But that was unnecessary, because an observation plane had already arrived on the scene. It made a wide circle then bounced to a landing in the field. Two men ran from the plane to the capsule and opened it. Out jumped Belka and Strelka, who appeared so grateful to be back on earth that they barked happily, ran around the field, jumping on everyone. It was a moment for the history books. They had become the first living creatures to be successfully returned to earth from orbit. At the launch site, everyone had been anxiously awaiting that news. When it came in, they cheered, shook hands, and hugged each other.

A few days later, at a press conference, reporters crowded around the two most famous dogs in the world. Belka barked a greeting into a microphone. The man with the thick glasses held both dogs over head for the crowd to see. These two dogs had just proven to the world that space travel was possible. They had brought the prospect of manned flight that much closer to reality. It was the proudest moment of the man's life and the most exciting moment in the space dog program.

Like Laika, Belka and Strelka achieved considerable worldwide fame. Newspapers around the world carried the story of their flight. Many countries honored them on post cards and postage stamps.

Although neither of these dogs would fly again, they continued to make contributions to the space program, and even played a role in international politics and keeping alive the memory of the exciting early days of space exploration.

Belka and Strelka became famous after becoming the first living creatures to return safely from space in 1960. *Novosti (London).*

The film made of Belka and Strelka in flight became a valuable training tool for the cosmonauts who would follow them into space.

They could see firsthand the flight conditions they would soon face. The film revealed how frightened the dogs looked during launch. It showed how strongly they had resisted the build up of g-forces, before the increasing acceleration eventually forced them to lay down. In the weightlessness of orbit, the dogs had floated stiff in air until they adjusted to the unusual experience of being without gravity.

Pushinka (right), the daughter of the famous space dog Strelka, grew up in the White House. She was given to President John Kennedy by Soviet Premier Nikita Khrushchev. Charlie, the other Kennedy dog pictured here, fathered a litter of pups with Pushinka. Those pups were given away to several children around the U.S.
Robert Knudsen, White House, John F. Kennedy Library.

Strelka even did her part to ease the political tension between the US and the Soviet Union when one of her puppies was given as a present to President John Kennedy. According to Ken O'Donnell, in his book, *Johnny, We Hardly Knew Ye*, the scene unfolded like this. The President and Mrs. Kennedy were in their apartment at the White House, when the Soviet ambassador appeared bearing a nervous, fluffy, white puppy. He explained that it was the daughter of Strelka, one of the dogs who had flown in space and that it was a gift from the Soviet premier to President Kennedy. It's name was Pushinka. The President stared at the dog and then at his wife, Jackie. She was holding her hand over her mouth in surprise. She whispered to the President, "I was only trying to make conversation." Apparently, a short time before, at a state dinner in Vienna, Jackie had asked the Soviet leader, Nikita Khrushchev about the space dogs. One of them had just had puppies, he told her. Jackie had said, "Why don't you send me one." So, that's exactly what he had done. Pushinka herself later had puppies, which were given away to children around the U.S.

Upon their deaths, Belka and Strelka were both stuffed and put on display at the Memorial Museum of Cosmonautics, in Moscow, where they remain to this day.

9

Space Dogs Finish Their Work

Some nights right after the Belka-Strelka flight, the man with the thick glasses would be so excited that he couldn't sleep. After tossing in his bed for a few hours, he'd rise and take Smelaya for a walk. Sometimes, if the night was clear, he'd place a chair in his backyard, put Smelaya in his lap, and stare at the stars. He would wave his hand overhead where Laika's orbit had crossed the sky, then again to draw a line where Belka and Strelka had passed. Old droopy ear would turn her head back and forth as though looking for a satellite, and the man would laugh.

Soviet scientists were just as excited about the Belka and Strelka flight. Because everything had worked so well, they immediately put together a schedule of flights for the next few months that would lead to the launch of the first human into space. The United States had announced that it would not be ready for its first suborbital manned flight until the spring of 1961, but the Soviets had already decided not to even attempt a human suborbital flight. They felt so confident in what they had learned from the dog flights that they planned to go directly to an orbital flight. They set as their goal to orbit a human before the U.S. could make even its first *suborbital* flight. They hoped to do this by late December 1960. Scientists only needed two more orbital flights with space dogs aboard to test new equipment and run more experiments. Given the wonderful success of the Belka-Strelka flight, this ambitious scheduled seemed reasonable. If the next two flights went smoothly, they would be able to pull it off.

The launch on December 1, with the space dogs Pchelka and Mushka on board, was just the sort of picture perfect flight they had hoped for. The dogs went into orbit at some 124 miles, the exact orbit planned for the first manned flight. After they circled the earth for one day, the command was radioed up for the rocket to fire, slow the capsule, and bring it back to earth. The man with the thick glasses held his breath for this critical maneuver. Not too slow, not too fast, the capsule had to slice back into the atmosphere at the perfect angle and speed.

The man stood behind one of the workers, watching the dogs on a TV screen. He had to tilt up his head and view it at just the right angle through his glasses to bring it into focus. The black and white images fluttered on the screen, painted with scratchy lines and fuzzy around the edges. But he could clearly make out Mushka's head. And there, Pchelka's as well. They looked around, alert, apparently doing well.

As the dogs began their descent, he focused his attention more carefully on the grainy TV images. Very little information existed about how a body reacted during reentry from orbit; this would be valuable information to the first human cosmonauts. He paused to scribble a note on his clipboard and when he turned back, the TV screen was blank. Sometimes the transmission got interrupted. He was not too concerned, until someone shouted, "Nothing on radar!"

"Nothing here either,"someone else yelled.

The man took a deep breath. Across the room an engineer caught his eye and used a fist to motion how the capsule had descended. His hand arched slowly downward, then violently snapped open. The man knew exactly what he meant. He threw down his clipboard and stormed from the room.

Moscow announced its official explanation to the world—The capsule had descended too fast and burned up in the atmosphere. However, that was a lie designed to hide the embarrassing truth. In the early days of the space dog program, everything had been done in complete secrecy. Only a handful of scientists and politicians ever learned about accidents and mistakes. But after the first two Sputnik flights, the whole world knew about the Soviet space program. Much publicity surrounded the flights, and mistakes were harder to hide.

The truth of what really happened on the Pchelka-Mushka flight would only be revealed many years later. The onboard rockets did indeed misfire and sent the capsule into a wrong angle of descent. But that did not cause the capsule to burn up in the atmosphere. Instead, these two space dogs were the victims of a secret device installed on all of the flights in those years. Because of the extreme secrecy that surrounded the missile and space program, Soviet scientists were very concerned about their spacecraft falling into the hands of foreign governments. For instance, if the capsule landed outside their borders, foreign governments might be able to retrieve the capsule and learn its secrets. The only sure way to prevent this from happening was to install an explosive device on all of its space craft that would explode automatically if the craft went off course.

Although such a device would not be onboard any of the manned flights, it was part of all the capsules that carried space dogs. As Pchelka and Mushka's capsule fell out of orbit and began reentry, a device onboard detected that it was off course and would land outside Soviet territory. It immediately sent a signal to the explosive device, and the capsule was destroyed, along with its crew.

This accident put the launch of the first human behind schedule. Improvements were quickly made to the rockets that had caused the problem, and three weeks later, on December 22, another rocket stood on the launch pad, with the space dogs Kometa and Shutka aboard. But this flight too would have its mechanical problems and turn into the most hair-raising dog flight of them all.

As the rocket was lifting these two dogs towards orbit, its third stage rocket malfunctioned. The emergency escape system shot the capsule free of the rocket and it landed in one of the most remote and inaccessible region of the Soviet Union, in Siberia, about 3,000 miles from the launch site.

The man with the thick glasses immediately pulled together a dog rescue team, a veterinarian, and two of the handlers who knew the dogs. They got a ride on a military aircraft and began the very long flight to Siberia. Although the man expected Pchelka and Mushka to have been rescued by the time he arrived, he would take possession of the dogs, give them any medical treatment they might need, and bring them home.

As soon as the flight cleared the runway, the man took out a notebook, checked his watch, then wrote, "55 hours, 18 minutes." Later that day they received a radio message that rescue crews in Siberia had detected radio signals from the downed capsule, allowing them to begin to pin point its location. The man checked his watch again, opened his notebook, and wrote "50 hours, 2 minutes–signals from capsule." The man breathed a sigh of relief. That was welcome news indeed. But the drama of this flight had just begun.

As with previous flights, this one also carried an automatic explosive device to protect the capsule from falling into foreign hands. In fact all of these flights carried *two* explosive devices. One blew up if the capsule went off course, and the other—connected to a timer—blew up if the rescue crew could not find the capsule within 60 hours. Ten hours had already passed. If a rescue crew did not arrive on the scene within the next 50 hours and disarm the explosive charge, the capsule and its space dog crew would be destroyed.

Each time the plane landed to refuel along the route, the man with the thick glasses got full updates on the search. Planes were crisscrossing the possible landing site, but the area was vast and it would take time, he learned at one stop. "Time is the one thing we don't have. 43 hours, 12 minutes," he scribbled in his notebook. At another refueling stop, he learned that a crew had been put on the ground in the approximate area. They reported waist-deep snow and bitterly cold temperatures. "A danger I hadn't thought of," he wrote, "that they might freeze to death before we reached them. 35 hours, 8 minutes."

His plane had to fly around a snow storm and wait for minor repairs. At each stop, he paced the airport runway to work off the rising tension he felt. He hadn't trained these dogs for years and launched them in a rocket to lose them in this way. They had to get their fast!

When he finally arrived at the airport from which the search was being coordinated, only seven hours remained before the explosive device would destroy the capsule. Grid squares had been drawn on a map of the area. An "X" marked the spot where a plane had picked up a faint radio signal from the capsule. The aerial search had expanded from there.

Late in the day, word finally came from one of the search planes that it had spotted the capsule. The man with the thick glasses rushed his team onto a helicopter and headed for the site.

A half hour into the flight, the man stared at his watch as it ticked off the final minute of the 60th hour. Which meant that they would not find the capsule but only bits and pieces of wreckage.

No one spoke a word for the rest of the flight, until they arrived at the location. "It's still there!" someone yelled. They all rushed to the window to look out. Sure enough, half buried in snow, the capsule lay there all in one piece. The explosive charge had not gone off.

They swarmed to the capsule. The capsule carrying the dogs had not separated from the rest of the space craft as it should have. That prevented the dogs from being easily removed. But first things first. They had to disarm the explosives. Either the timer was not working properly and they might all be blown to bits at any second or it had been damaged. Either way the delicate job of disconnecting the explosives had to happen before they tried to remove the dogs.

The temperature stood at a bitter -40 degrees. The helicopter pilot could not turn off his engine for fear that it would freeze up and not start again, leaving them stranded in this frigid wilderness. The men worked as quickly as possible in their bulky gloves, wrestling with the damaged pieces of the space craft until they could reach the explosives.

Finally, they were successful and could begin to remove the dogs. But, by then darkness was setting in. "We have to return right now," the pilot insisted. He was low on fuel and could not fly at night in this unfamiliar territory.

The man with the thick glasses rubbed frost away from the small glass port hole and knocked on the capsule but could not see the dogs or hear them bark. He could not determine if they were still alive. They would be on their own for one more night.

At first light the helicopter returned the men to the capsule. The temperature had fallen to -49 degrees over night. Flesh froze to metal at the merest touch. Could the dogs have survived? They soon had their answer. As they began to remove the container from the space-craft, the dogs began to bark. The man with the thick glasses removed his heavy sheepskin coat and wrapped it around the dogs. They had survived their rocket flight and the more challenging ordeal of recovery.

The problems with those two December flights, pushed back a launch date for a manned flight. Two more space dogs would travel in space before a human cosmonaut would fly. On March 9, 1961, a space dog named Chernushka (Blackie) circled the earth for one orbit, along with a guinea pig, some mice and a wooden dummy of a cosmonaut, given the name Ivan Ivanovich. The flight went smoothly, the dummy was ejected from the capsule and recovered by parachute, and Chernushka was recovered successfully with the capsule.

On March 25, in what would be a final rehearsal for a manned flight, a space dog once again paired up with the wooden cosmonaut Ivan Ivanovich, for the one-orbit flight of *Sputnik 10*. Again, the dummy was ejected from the capsule and recovered by parachute, and Zvezdochka was recovered with the capsule.

Three days after Zvezdochka's successful return, Soviet officials held a press conference in Moscow, at the Soviet Academy of Science. They showed off Zvezdochka, the most recent in a line of successful canine cosmonauts. Dozens of reporters crowded in to snap photos of the heroic pooch. But this moment was not for Zvezdochka alone. Chernushka, Belka, and Strelka were also on hand to share the moment of glory. They stood calmly by, accepting the worshipful attention of the reporters. They were the "even-tempered" dogs, the ones that had been marked for fame from that moment when the first dogs were recruited for the space program. Now they stood together, having accomplished their mission and made their contribution to the science of space flight. They had led the way into space, and now humans could follow in their footsteps.

Space dogs Chernushka (Blackie) and Zvezdochka (Little Star), who both made successful orbital flights in March of 1961, are introduced to the public at a press conference. *Novosti (London).*

In case the impact of the moment had escaped anyone, in case that group of cute and cuddly celebrities was not enough to melt the public's heart, one more surprise awaited. Strelka had been pregnant during her orbital flight and had recently given birth to a litter of pups.

Out they came, put on stage with these heroines of the Soviet space program. What better way to demonstrate that space travel was safe than to show off four veteran space travelers and their healthy off-spring?

That March 1961 press conference marked a turning point. There was no grand announcement that the days of the space dogs were over and that humans would now take their place, but that very prospect hung in the air. Soviet scientists had been pleased with the performance of Sputnik 9 and 10. They had solved the problems with their space craft and its recovery, and answered any lingering questions about the safety of space flight. Space dogs would be called back into service just one more time before their program was closed down for good, but the time had come now for human space flight to begin.

On April 12, 1961, less than three weeks after Zvezdochka's flight, the Soviet Union launched the first human being into space. Cosmonaut Yuri Gagarin successfully completed one orbit and returned safely to earth to become the hero of the Soviet space program and an international celebrity.

The final chapter in the history of space dogs occurred five years later. Focus had now shifted to long-term flights in space, and once again space dogs would take the first step. On February 22, 1966, space dogs Veterok (Little Wind) and Ugolek (Little Piece of Coal) flew aboard the satellite Cosmos 110 for a record 22 days in orbit. They had no problems during the flight and landed safely on March 15. Their flight is still the canine flight record. Humans would not achieve a space flight that long for eight more years, in Skylab 2.

But apparently space still had a few mysteries to unravel. Shortly after the flight, Veterok lost his hair and energy and died soon afterward. Ugolek, on the other hand, survived and experienced a considerable increase in energy, including an urge to father a lot of puppies. Ugolek's stuffed body is on display at the Russian Institute of Biomedical Problems.

Epilogue
November 1997

A cold wind blew hard into the faces of the small crowd standing outside the offices of the Institute for Aviation and Space Medicine, in Star City, outside of Moscow. They had gathered to dedicate a monument to the pioneers of the Soviet space program, those brave cosmonauts who had paid the highest price and given their lives in the interest of science.

A few somber speeches set the tone for the occasion. Forty years had passed, they explained, since the exploration of space had taken the life of the small, mongrel dog named Laika. Others who had dedicated themselves to this noble cause, had fallen since then. This monument is dedicated to their sacrifice. When the cloth was dropped from the monument, someone read the names of the men who had lost their lives.

An old man stood far back from the crowd, bundled in a winter coat, scarf, and hat. When the last speech had been delivered and the people hurried back into the warmth of the building, the old man approached the monument. He studied it carefully, appreciatively. Finally, he took a pair of thick glasses from his inside pocket, propped them onto his nose, and peered down at the plaque that bore the image of the space dog Laika. His fingers reached out to rub the familiar image, and he was instantly flooded with a hundred memories of the space dog program.

This was a fine monument to Laika, but he knew that she was but one of the many dogs who gave their lives, and one of the many who flew on rockets to teach humans what they needed to know to explore space. Who now remembered them? A parade of fuzzy faces danced in his memory—Tsygan and Dezik, the first to fly; Lisa and Dezik, the first to die. Those early dogs, who flew in such secrecy that all of their names had not been recorded. Brave Smelaya scooped from the streets of Moscow; dark Chernushka spinning in the centrifuge. He saw them all. Ugolek and Veterok, circling in space for 22 days.

How could you honor them all, but to repeat their names? Which is exactly what he did, in a voice so strong it carried on the wind. "Tsygan, Dezik, Lisa, Mishka, Chizhik, Smelaya, Ryzhik, Neputevyy, and ZIB, Lisa 2, Damka, Albina, Tsyganka, Bulba, Malyshka, Knopka, and Kozyavka, Linda, Rzyhaya, Dzhoyna, Belka, Modnitsa, Laika, Kusachka, Palma, Belyanka, and Pestraya, Neva, Otvazhnaya, Snezhinka, Zemchuznaya, Malek, Chaika, Lisichka, Strelka, Pchelka, Mushka, Kometa, Shutka, Chernushka, Zvezdochka, Ugolek, and Veterok."

Flight Log
A record of those who flew

Records of the space dog flights are far from complete. The exact number of dog flights and even some launch dates are disputed by researchers. Records, especially for the early flights, do not always list the names of the dogs that flew. This list is my attempt to reconcile the conflicting facts. It is, in some cases, a "best guess." An asterisk*indicates when a dog died during the flight.

Flight Date	Space Dogs
7-22-51	Tsygan, Dezik
7-29-51	Lisa*, Dezik*
8-15-51	Mishka, Chizhik
8-19-51	Smelaya, Ryzhik
8-28-51	Mishka*, Chizhik*
9-3-51	Neputevyy, ZIB
7-2-54	Lisa-2, Ryzhik
7-7-54	Damka, Ryzhik
7-26-54	Lisa-2, Ryzhik*
1-25-55	Albina, Tsyganka
2-5-55	Lisa-2*, Bulba*
11-4-55	Malyshka, Knopka
5-14-56	Albina, Kozyavka
5-31-56	Malyshka, Linda
6-7-56	Albina, Kozyavka

5-16-57	Rzyhaya, Damka
5-24-57	Rzyhaya*, Dzhoyna*
8-25-57	Belka, Modnitsa
11-3-57	Laika*
8-2-58	Kusachka, Palma
8-13-58	Kusachka, Palma
8-27-58	Belyanka, Pestraya
9-17-58	2 dogs (Possibly Damka & Kozyavka)
10-31-58	2 dogs (Possibly Damka & Kozyavka)
7-2-59	Otvazhnaya, Snezhinka
7-10-59	Otvazhnaya, Zemchuznaya
6-15-60	Otvazhnaya, Malek
6-24-60	Otvazhnaya, Zemchuznaya
7-28-60	Chaika*, Lisichka*
8-19-60	Belka, Strelka
9-16-60	Palma, Malek
9-22-60	Otvazhnaya, Neva
12-1-60	Pchelka*, Mushka*
12-22-60	Kometa, Shutka
3-9-61	Chernushka
3-25-61	Zvezdochka
2-22-66	Ugolek, Veterok

Glossary

Acceleration—The rate of change in the speed of a moving body.

Astronaut—A person trained to fly aboard a rocket.

Baikonur—A rocket facility in the central part of the Russia (Soviet Union). Laika was launched from here.

Capsule—A space craft containing the crew of a rocket flight. It usually contained pressurized air to support the life of an astronaut or animal making high altitude or orbital flights.

Centrifuge—A machine with a long rotating arm. Humans or animals were revolved in a capsule at the end of this arm to simulate the increased force of gravity they would experience on a rocket flight.

Confinement capsule—A piece of training equipment designed to familiarize space dogs in training with what it would be like to be confined in a very small space, cut off from contact with the world, just what they would experience in a real rocket capsule.

Cosmonaut—A Soviet astronaut.

G or G-Force—A unit measuring the increasing force, or weight, experienced during acceleration. One "G" is equal to the gravitational pull of the earth.

Gravity—The force that pulls all things towards the center of the earth, giving them weight.

Kapustin Yar—A Soviet rocket facility located near the Caspian Sea.

Khrushchev, Nikita—Former leader (premier) of the Soviet Union.

Mesosphere—Layer of the atmosphere located about 34 to 50 miles above the Earth, where temperature decreases with higher altitude.

Moscow—The capitol of the Soviet Union.

Nose Cone—The cone-shaped tip of a rocket, usually containing instruments and/or live passengers.

Orbit—The path taken by a satellite or space craft as it moves around a planet.

Orbital Velocity—The speed at which an object must travel around a planet to stay in orbit. The orbital velocity of the Earth is 18,000 miles per hour.

Re-entry—The return of a rocket or space capsule into the atmosphere after it has been in space.

Rocket Dogs—Space dogs, selected because of their frisky personality, to go on the early, high-altitude rocket flights.

Rocket Sled—A sled that runs on rails and is powered by a rocket to very high speeds.

Satellite—A unpowered object in space which revolves about another body.

Satellite Dogs—Space dogs, selected because of their calm personality, to go on the longer flights, including those that orbited the earth.

Soviet Union—The former name for the country that is now Russia and some other countries that formed the USSR, Union of Soviet Socialist Republics.

Space Race—The competition between the United States and the Soviet Union to be the first to get into space and to achieve other accomplishments in the development of rockets and the exploration of space.

Space Suit—Clothing developed to allow living beings to function in space. It provided such necessary features as air for breathing, pressure to counter the vacuum of space, and would have attachments of wires for monitoring the body functions, and tubing to pass off waste materials. Other flight clothing designed to meet some of these same needs were called: sanitation suit, pressure suit, and flight suit.

Sputnik—The Russian name for its early satellites. The full Russian term is *Iskustvenyi Sputnik Zewli*, "artificial companion of the earth."

Stratosphere—Layer of the atmosphere from about 12 to 31 miles above the earth, where temperature increases with higher altitude.

Suborbital Flights—Rocket flights that went high in the atmosphere but did not go into orbit.

Thermosphere—Layer of the atmosphere beginning at about 53 miles above the earth, where there can be a very wide range in temperatures.

V-2 Rocket—The first large rocket capable of flights into the upper atmosphere. It was developed by Germany during World War II and later used by both the United States and the Soviet space programs.

Vibration machine/Vibration Table—A piece of training equipment for the space dogs. The dogs were placed on a small platform on top of this machine, which was then made to vibrate. This gave the dogs a feel for the vibrations they would experience during the launch of a rocket.

Weightlessness—The absence of any gravitational pull on an object, making it weightless.

Zero Gravity—Having no gravity and thus no weight, as experienced aboard a satellite in orbit around the Earth. Weightlessness.

Bibliography

Animals and Man in Space, A Chronology and Annotated Bibliography Through the Year 1960, Dietrich E. Beischer and Alfred R. Fegley. U.S. Naval School of Aviation Medicine, U.S. Naval Aviation Medical Center, Pensacola, FL, Office of Naval Research, Department of the Navy, Washington, DC.

Animals Astronauts, Clyde R. Bergwin and William T. Coleman. Prentice-Hall, Inc, Englewood Cliffs, NJ. 1963.

Behind the Sputniks, a Survey of Soviet Space Science, F.J. Krieger. Public Affairs Press, Washington, DC. 1958.

Challenge to Apollo, The Soviet Union and the Space Race, 1945-1974, Asif A. Siddiq. NASA, Washington, DC. 2000.

Handbook of Soviet Space Science Research, George E. Wukelic, ed. Gordon and Breach Science Publishers, NY. 1968.

The First Astronauts and the First Scouts of Outer Space, M.A. Gerd and N.N. Gurovskiy. Izdatel'stvo Akademii Nauk, SSSR, Moskva 1962. Prepared by the Translation Division, Foreign Technology Division, WP-AFB, Ohio.

"Johnny, We Hardly Knew Ye;" Memories of John Fitzgerald Kennedy, Kenneth P. O'Donnell and David F. Powers, with Joe McCarthy. Little Brown, Boston. 1972.

Korolev, How One Man Masterminded the Soviet Drive to Beat America to the Moon, James Harford. John Wiley & Sons, Inc., NY. 1997

Red Star in Orbit, James E. Oberg. Random House, NY. 1981.

Roads to Space, An Oral History of the Soviet Space Program, Compiled by the Russian Scientific Research Center for Space Documentation, Translated by Peter Berlin, Edited by John Rhea. Aviation Week Group, McGraw-Hill. 1995.

Russians in Space, Evgeny Riabchikov, Edited by Colonel General Nikolai P. Kamanin, Translated by Guy Daniels. Doubleday & Company, Inc. Garden City, NY. 1971.

The Use of Nonhuman Primates in Space, Proceedings of a Symposium held at Ames Research Center, Moffett Field, CA. December 2–4, 1974.

CPSIA information can be obtained at www.ICGtesting.com
Printed in the USA
LVOW08s1816141214

418776LV00004B/305/P

9 780595 267354